A
Hiawatha Island
Childhood
1911 — 1919

A
Hiawatha Island
Childhood
1911 — 1919

Eupha M. Shanly

*Illustrated with related photographs, drawings,
engravings and advertisements from the era, plus numerous
front covers of sheet music then popular.*

Sned Books
Blanchester, Ohio

Sned Books
219 N. Mill St.
Blanchester, Ohio 45107-1142

99   98   97   2   3   4   5   6   7

Library of Congress Cataloging–in–Publication Data

Shanly, Eupha M.
    A Hiawatha Island Childhood, 1911 - 1919/ Eupha M.
Shanly -- 1st ed.
        p.   cm.
    ISBN 1-882203-19-4
    1. Hiawatha Island (Tioga County, N.Y.)--Social life and
customs.   2. Country life--New York (State)--Hiawatha
Island (Tioga County)   3. Shanly, Eupha M.--Childhood
and youth.   4. Hiawatha Island (Tioga County, N.Y.)--
Biography.   I. Title.
F127.S96S53   1998
974.7'77--dc21   97-52107
                                                 CIP

Book and Cover design: Tom Hawley, Marblehead, MA

On the Cover:
1911 photo of the author, cozy in sheepskins, enjoying a
sled ride on river ice by Hiawatha Island. The family
collie, Bingo, stayed close by.

To My Parents
Lynn W. and Mertie L. Snedaker
Who by their Example
Prepared Me
For the
GLORIOUS
ADVENTURE
That Is
LIFE

I've traveled far to rendezvous with age.
Varied goals have set the changing stage.
Drama does not end. While memory is bright,
I write. — EMS

Contents

Acknowledgments

My late husband, John Stuart Shanly, who loved books. He gave moral support to my efforts and, over a decade ago, convinced me to replace the typewriter with a computer.

My brother, the Reverend L. Elmo Snedaker and his family.

My nieces and nephews, Mary Janeth Scanlon and Scott A. Smith, Verna's surviving children; Mark C. Snedaker, Charles L. Snedaker, and Cathy Warner, Carl's surviving children.

My own children and grandchildren, especially Tom Roskelly and his wife, Caren Belli.

The staffs of the Blanchester, Wilmington, and Dayton, Ohio Public Libraries.

My invaluable friend, Becky L. Howard. She comes at least once a week to make sure my laundry is done, the floors clean, the garden weeded and watered. Then we break bread together.

Darrel Burkhart, former editor of *Susquehanna, The Sunday Magazine,* in Binghamton, New York. He published my *Growing Up on Hiawatha Island* story on Mother's Day, May 13, 1979.

Emma M. Sedore, who demonstrated that many people are interested in Island lore. I refrained from reading her work until this manuscript was finished. She researched and wrote *Hiawatha Island, Jewel of the Susquehanna,* ©. 1994 — a superb job.

All the authors whose books through the years have invited me to share their knowledge and insights, and continue to please me.

A
Hiawatha Island
Childhood
1911 — 1919

CHAPTER 1

Way Back When

The Susquehanna is one of the most ancient rivers of the North American continent and its watershed extends westward to that of the Mississippi River System. The river bed beneath Chesapeake Bay provides proof that it originally emptied directly into the Atlantic, before the bay itself was formed.

Unlike the rivers of the coastal plain, its general direction of flow is southward. Rising in what is now New York State, it traverses 440 miles, bisecting Pennsylvania and reaching its greatest width in Maryland. The Algonquins and later the Iroquois and people of the Six Nations of their confederacy, moved swiftly and silently in birch bark canoes over the waters of its tributaries.

A natural fortress with a garrison of eight hundred warriors at the Indian Village of Carantouan on the Chemung, a Susquehanna tributary, was widely known. Tradition tells of Spaniards from DeSoto's Expedition making the long trek to the northeast to see it. From this story comes its name, Spanish Hill. They were probably the first Europeans to visit the Susquehanna Territory.

Samuel de Champlain accompanied an exploring and fur–trading expedition up the St. Lawrence River to the Lachine Rapids, under orders from Henry IV of France. He heard of Carantouan and sent Stephen Brule to scout it out in 1603. Brule was gone three years, having survived capture by a war party. As they started to torture him, a thunderstorm of such intensity that the Indians believed it an omen, not only freed Brule and his party, but won them every assistance as they returned to Canada.

A group of German canoeists floated down the Susquehanna from Otsego Lake to southern Pennsylvania in 1723.

In 1743, John Bartram came from Philadelphia to botanize. He tarried at the Indian village standing on the present site of Owego. I like to imagine him visiting Hiawatha Island to collect seeds and possibly saplings for his garden back home. That garden, which Benjamin Franklin and George Washington enjoyed in their time., is now part of Philadelphia's park system. Many of its giant trees were Bartram–planted. Twenty–two years later, William Bartram, the son, visited the area again. Both kept excellent journals.

My Snedaker and Rockwell forebears were among the European pioneers who followed its valley, from their early settlements near the ocean to the unbroken wilderness extending westward from the Delaware River.

During the Clinton–Sullivan punitive expedition of the Revolutionary War, Clinton's army built boats at Otsego Lake, the headwaters of the Susquehanna, and floated their supplies to meet Sullivan's augmented forces near today's Athens, Pennsylvania. The supplies went by water but the men walked the whole distance through the present towns of Owego, Nichols, Tioga, and Barton. They were impressed with the valley and after the war, many moved their families here from New England.

Even the future Citizen King of France, Louis–Philippe, son of the guillotined duc d'Orleans, explored the Susquehanna with his two younger brothers and a servant during 1796–97. They went on horseback from Philadelphia to Baltimore by way of Havre De Grace which, before 1785, was known as Susquehanna Lower Ferry. They had a rough crossing but continued on their grand tour going west and north through Kentucky to Ohio and the Great Lakes. The royal diary tells of Niagara and the Genessee Valley. They continued their great circle by canoe, down the Susquehanna, through this area, as far as today's Wilkes–Barre, PA.

Today's Susquehanna is less widely known. It is shallow. Louis–Philppe's diary mentioned, " . . . the recently begun canal to bypass the falls of the Susquehanna," near its mouth. Early settlers built dams to power their saw and grist mills, one just south of Lanesboro, but the river's long valleys and gentle grades invited the building of turnpikes, shunpikes, and railroads early on.

Cooperstown •

Oneonta •

Owego •   Binghamton •

New York

Hiawatha Island

Sayre •
Athens •

Lanesboro •

West
Branch
Susquehanna

Scranton •

Kingston •
Wilkes-Barre •

• Sunbury

Pennsylvania

Harrisburg
•

Susquehanna
River

N

W   E

S

Maryland

Havre
de Grace •

Chesapeake Bay

More than a century ago, the Erie instituted rail–river excursions. They teamed up with steamboat owners in Owego and also in Pennsylvania, bringing hordes of visitors to Big Island, later renamed Hiawatha, for gala picnics and weekend gaiety. Owego's *Lyman Truman* and the earlier Owego steamboats are part of the Island's saga.

W. G. Briggs investigated the Lanesboro story. C. M. Harding, a photographer from the Borough of Susquehanna, had honed his keen memory for over ninety years. He remembered Ben Pride, publisher of *The Susquehanna, (PA) Journal.* In about 1880, Ben's brother, Fred Pride, bought and refurbished two steamboats; the double–decker *Erminie*, with a capacity of 250 passengers, and her smaller sister, *Idlewild*, which towed a popular dance floor on a barge.

In the December 1954 issue of *Courier Magazine*, published in Deposit, Briggs recounts a tale of the *Erminie's* fireman. Lacking "incandescent light," he read the steam gauge on the boiler at night by using a glowing red–hot poker.

The article carried a photo done in the '80's on wet plate by

Sneduker farm on Hiawatha Island, July 1917

Martin Pooler. It shows the *Erminie,* with its vacationing throng enjoying a view of the multiple–arched Starucca viaduct with a Binghamton–bound locomotive and cars passing over it.

Pride docked his two boats near Taylor's Grove which had its own dancing pavilion, merry–go–round, and refreshment stand, and was within walking distance of the Erie Depot. Sometimes the boats went only to Binghamton, other times all the way to the Island.. The larger boat burned at its dock around Christmas time in the winter of 1895–96 and the other passed the point of prof-itable repair, ending that era.

All this, of course, was long before my time. I like to reflect that long after my time, people will be enjoying the Island. It has now been designated a permanent nature conservancy connected with the Fred L. Waterman Conservation and Education Nature Center. Its year–round museum is located on Marshland Road on the Apalachin side of the river.

Wedding photo of Lynn and Mertie Barton Snedaker, April 16, 1900.

CHAPTER 2

A Bit About Us

Never doubt that one's name reveals something of one's family. Pilgrim parents in the early Massachusetts Bay colony named daughters Piety, Prudence, and other virtue names like Mercy, Humility, and Charity. One little girl answered to Hate–Evil, another to Kill–Sin

The story of my naming began long before my birth. The year of 1897 was a time of distress for my father, Lynn Snedaker. A week before his 30th birthday, "gallopin' consumption," then the common term for tuberculosis because of the speed with which it "consumed" its victims, took its toll. Dad was left bereft of his young wife, Elsie, and a still–born son. Bewildered by trying to care for his remaining children, five–year–old Harry and 26–month–old Verna in his grief, he stayed for a while with his parents. Harry proved too much for his 70–year–old Grandmother Snedaker, so Dad took him to live with his Snitchler grandparents on a farm near Hamilton, New York. Verna stayed at Ingraham Hill, near Binghamton. When the harvest was in and winter settled to cracking cold, Dad put on his warmest duds, took some extra warm work socks, shouldered his axe, and left for a Pennsylvania lumbering camp out McKeesport way. While a small farm could feed a family, a man needed hard cash for taxes and "boughten goods," so Father spent several winters that way.

One winter, he lived in a boarding house in Morristown, New Jersey. Cities were growing rapidly and crying for timber to build homes, factories, and stores. The woods were so near that the lumber company gave the men allowances for room and board and shut down their own bunk houses and camp kitchen. That was when Dad said he first found himself able to enjoy the company of small children. He watched them at play. His landlady called to her toddler grandchild, "Eupha, come in to supper now," and Dad decided it was high time to put his mourning behind him and get on with his life.

When spring started to soften the ground, horses could no longer drag out the felled trunks . The men collected their wages and headed for home. Only those who hired out their horses as well as their own labor rode back. The rest walked.

Tommy Barton of Vestal Center was one of the older men in the same crew as Dad. He and Dad paired off for the journey home. Dad stopped for the night with the Bartons. That was when he met Mertie, Tom's oldest daughter. They courted that summer and the following Easter Monday, April 16, 1990, they were married in the Methodist Church in Vestal Center. Mother started off with a ready–made family. She was used to caring for her younger brothers and sisters.

When they began a child of their own, Dad confided that he had just the name for a daughter. Mother liked his idea. Despite pressure from some of Elsie's distant cousins to name the baby for her, Mother said, "No. I don't believe in naming a brand new baby for a dead person." And she didn't. It was a boy. When told she should name him Cornelius, "because 'there's been a Cornelius every second generation,'" she kept just the initial, calling him Carl Charles Snedaker.

Mother had trouble with fibroid tumors and underwent surgery. It was almost eight years before she again felt life. Her doctor assured her that she was imagining things and it . . . "could be another tumor," . . . but tumors don't kick. Mother sought out the new doctor in Endicott, Dr. Mead.

Grandpa Barton died in October of 1906. Grandma still lived in Vestal Center and my parents a few miles away on Friendsville stage road. Grandma hitched the mare to the buggy and came in a hurry when mother phoned that her pains had started, for Dad was staying in town that week, working. Mother asked the telephone operator to leave a line open to Endicott when she closed the switchboard for the night . . . a wise precaution. A few hours later,

Dr. Roger Mead was on his way. I was born September 1, 1910. Dad was 41 years old and Mother 30. Harry was 19, Verna 16, and Carl eight at the time.

Four-story Hiawatha House from a postcard, as it appeared in 1911.

When Dad came in, he heard a baby's cry and rushed to Mother's bedside. Yes, she was fine and the baby certainly was . . . I had good lungs from all reports. "So, what did you name her?"

"Eupha Mae."

Dad swallowed hard. "Where did that come from?"

Mother laughed, "Why Lynn, you've forgotten Morristown!"

I have no memory of the bragging trip Dad made with his family to introduce me to his former landlady. "We named her for your granddaughter," he announced.

She gathered me into her arms for a big hug. "Let me look at you, Euphemia," and she hugged me again.

My name is still Eupha. I use the middle initial to keep people from thinking I'm Euphas Hanly.

Harry, Verna and Carl Snedaker, 1904

The Island family, Lynn, Carl, Eupha and Mertie Snedaker. a.1919

CHAPTER 3

The Snedaker Siblings
vs.
The World

Harry and Verna were born in the Gay Nineties; Carl in the first decade of the Twentieth Century; Eupha, and Elmo in the second decade, 1910 and 1919.

Harry rebelled against the world and manipulated it.

Verna dreamed and danced through it.

Carl had to find out how it worked.

Eupha explored and enjoyed it.

Elmo was concerned about the health of the earth and ministered to its people.

From *Song of Hiawatha*

Thus the Birch Canoe was builded
In the valley, by the river,
In the bosom of the forest;
And the forest life was in it,
All its mystery and its magic,
all the lightness of the birch tree,
All the toughness of the cedar,
All the larch's supple sinews;
and it floated on the river
Like a yellow leaf in autumn,
Like a yellow water lily.

HENRY W. LONGFELLOW

CHAPTER 4

My Pretty Little Boat

Decades before, birch bark canoes pulled onto the island's banks as powerful Indian leaders from most of the northern watershed of the Susquehanna arrived, paddling down its many tributaries. Legend tells that a charismatic visionary, Hiawatha, summoned them that they might form bonds of cooperation and peace rather than war among themselves. Five tribes made up the original Iroquois League. Later, a sixth was added and several smaller tribes adopted into the Mohawks and Senecas. The League is historic fact, but the legend is not reliable as to time and place.

Each winter we lived on Hiawatha Island, Dad built a boat: a rowboat. Three or four were kept at the landing during open–water season. They were the only dry way to get to the mainland unless we hand–pulled the vehicle–carrying ferry. Canoes were for vacationers. We never owned one.

After the bulk of the field work was finished and winter closed down, the river ice thickened. Boats were pulled from the water, inspected, and stored upside down, well above the high–water mark until next spring's recaulking and repainting. Then it was time for new projects.

It was only natural for Dad, who spent most of his working years in timbering or construction with farming on the side, to get intense personal satisfaction from building useful objects of wood. When the IBM behemoth began its evolution from Bundy Manufacturing, it first metamorphosed into the International Time Recording Company (ITR), and sold off a lot of Seth Thomas eight–day pendulum clock works, a dozen or so to my father. That particular winter, he built handsome walnut shelf–clock cases and hand–carved the frames of the clock faces and arched area above their glass doors. Today's generation of our extended family prize them highly and wind them weekly.

Even that winter, he still managed time to build a boat, drawing the plans and selecting the stock carefully. Throughout the sawing, planing, shaping (partly by steaming, as I recall), the dovetailing, gluing, nailing and bradding, clamping and sanding, he proceeded with his work easily and happily, a true artisan. The length of the oar blade had to be in proportion to the dimensions of the boat. All the metal fittings, such as the oarlocks, were chosen with a practiced eye. The boat bottom tilted upward gradually toward the bow and the rear was reinforced inside and out with heavy cleats to withstand the bumping and scraping incidental to normal use. The rocks of the Susquehanna are not the sand–scoured, wave–eroded beach pebbles of salty marine waters, and each time a boat here was beached, it was dragged half out of the water and chained to a secure post or sturdy tree.

Most of Dad's boats had three seats, the widest thwart for the rower or side–by–side rowers, another across the back, and a triangular one at the bow. Kid–like, I thought of the removable slat sections between thwarts as false floors, but they had the utilitarian virtue of keeping one's feet dry. When the normal bilge became deep enough to slosh or float them, we'd tip up the sections and bail with rusty old cans kept at hand for that purpose.

Boat seams were caulked with oakum, the fibers of old rope, untwisted. This was part of maintenance as well. Then the boat was submerged, held down with large stones — boulders was a term I never knew until I started to read — and left to swell watertight.

Dad was well aware in the winter of 1914 – 15, that his little girl would start going to Owego to attend kindergarten in September. At that point in my life, I was small for my age. Mother told of buying doll's shoes for me when I started walking. As I tried to clamber onto a chair seat, somebody would often swing me off my feet and set me in place. "Light as air," they'd laugh.

Dad worked in his self-built shop, a sturdy poured–concrete affair with lumber in the loft, a forge at one side, large workbench and a multitude of tools which he kept in a fabulous toolbox. It was cozy, even during our Tioga County winters, heated by a wood–burning stove which also consumed shavings, sawdust, and small wood scraps. This boat was somehow different, but not until it was completed and painted a heavenly blue did I realize it was sized for me. It was narrow and barely five feet long. Even little oars, were just my size.

Winter waned and Dad was as anxious as I to try out my little boat. The main body of river ice had passed, swept away in a thaw flood towards the Chesapeake, but floes and a considerable amount of shore–stranded pans were plentiful when our patience finally ran thin.

Dad called from the landing and Mother and I went down. He wore a Cheshire cat grin. "Get in, Mertie," he invited and she sat down on the wide end seat with me on her lap. Dad stepped in . .

. and the boat sank! Too much weight for volume displacement. I can still feel that icy water coming up my legs and over the seat as we giggled and jumped to shore.

That miniature boat was my delight and my Grandmother Newcomb's nightmare. I doubt she ever approved of my being out on the river playing when she wasn't even sure I could swim. Had Mother and Dad been worrying types, they'd have turned white–haired or bald far before their time!

Once, when Grandma came by train to visit us, she called from the far shore. Everyone else was busy in the fields, so Mother sent me across the river to fetch her. I rowed very well and knew my way across for that is how I got to the mainland every day to catch the school wagon during the week. One had to let the boat slant downstream a bit to avoid a sometime submerged sand bar which altered its shape and location with every passing flood. I knew where it was all right, but Grandmother thought I wasn't strong enough to keep a straight course.

As soon as we were safely past, I pulled harder on one oar and brought the boat to a perfect landing. "There," I said cheerfully, fastening the boat chain to the post, "wasn't that fun? Oh, I do love to row."

Color started coming back into Grandma's knuckles as she finally loosened her clutch on the boat's side, but for the life of me I can't remember her answering.

SWIFT'S VERSES ON
"THE VOWELS."

We are little airy creatures,
All of different sound and
features;
One of us in glass is set,
One of us is found in jet;
T'other you may see in tin,
And the fourth a box within;
If the fifth you should pursue,
It can never fly from you.

CHAPTER 5

School Time and Games

For three years I was the youngest and smallest child on the school wagon. All children through high school seniors were transported, and kids were getting on or off all along the way. Despite that, we played lots of guessing or identification games to pass the time.

I look back on how graciously the older kids included me. They eased the rules now and then. Who cared who won or lost? The fun was in the playing.

Buzz and Fizz kept me thinking all the time. In Buzz, we simply counted off around the long plank seats, up one side and down the other, substituting the word "buzz" for any five or multiple of five. ONE — TWO— THREE— FOUR — BUZZ — SIX — that's how it should go. I listened and soon learned to count by fives. Fifty–five was "buzz – buzz," of course.

Fizz was harder. It was based on the digit seven and its multiples . . . seven, fourteen, seventeen, twenty–one, twenty–seven, twenty–eight — all were Fizz I got lost in a hurry when they started Buzz–Fizz, dealing with both numbers and names — Buzz for fives and Fizz for sevens, and I seldom got past Fizz (27)! The number 28 was another Fizz, 29 wasn't and 30 was . Thirty-five, being the multiple of both 5 and 7, was Buzz–Fizz, and so was 57 because of the digits. After 69, one could scarcely keep track if wearing mittens because of 70, 75, and 77 being doubled-named.

Rhymed guessing games worked well on the sleigh in winter. "I'm thinking of something that rhymes with meal."

> "Is it part of your foot?"
> "No, it's not my heel."
> "Is it an animal that swims?"

"No, it isn't a seal."

"Is it part of a wagon?"

"YES! It's a wheel!"

Once I stuck them all with, "I spy, with my little eye, something that's way up high!" They guessed the top of a tall tree, a barn roof, the sun, the moon and stars, the sky, clouds, a flying bird, and finally gave up. It was a lightning rod. The valley had severe thunder storms, so most houses and barns sported them, and church steeples, too.

On the way to school, as more children got on, my turn came less and less often.

At school recess, we played singing games like The Farmer in the Dell. Teacher picked a farmer to stand in the center of the circle, while the rest clasped hands and sang:

> The farmer in the dell, the farmer in the dell
> High–ho, the Derry–O, the farmer in the dell.
> The farmer takes a wife, the farmer takes a wife
> High–ho, the Derry–O, the farmer takes a wife.

The farmer chose his wife to join him, and the circling continued, with another child chosen in each verse.

> The wife takes a child . . .
> The child takes a nurse . . .
> The nurse takes a dog . . .
> The dog takes a cat . . .
> The cat takes a mouse . . .
> The mouse takes the cheese . . .
> The cheese stands alone . . .

Then everyone dropped hands and ran to re-form the circle, leaving the cheese in the center to be the new farmer.

London Bridge had enough singing and shouting to get it out of our systems. Preventive discipline, as it were. The tallest two faced each other, arms high and arched. The rest passed through, single file, until the end of the verse when the bridge–keepers tried to cage a victim. We struggled or dodged, but when caught, started forming for a final tug–of–war, behind the cagers, hands around each other's waists.

London Bridge is falling down, falling down, falling down.
London Bridge is falling down, my Fair Laaaady.
Build it back with wood and clay, wood and clay, wood and clay
Build it back with wood and clay, My Fair Laaaady.
Wood and clay will wash away, wash away, wash away.
Wood and clay will wash away, My Fair Laaaady.

Other verses followed the same rhythm:

Build it up with iron and steel . . .
Iron and steel will bend and break . . .
Build it up with silver and gold . . .
Silver and gold will be stolen away . . .
Hire a man to watch all night . . .
Suppose the man should fall asleep . . .
Take the keys and lock him up . . .

DIRECTIONS FOR LONDON BRIDGE

Two children make the bridge by raising their arms so as to form an arch: the others form a line, each one holding onto the waist of the child in front of him, and they pass under the arch.

At the words, "My Fair Lady," the two who form the bridge let their arms fall, catching whichever child happens to be passing. He is then asked, "Which do you prefer, gold or silver?" and he is sent behind one or the other of the bridge–makers according to his choice (they having previously agreed who will stand for silver and who for gold).

After all have chosen, the game ends with a tug–of–war between the two sides.

Tag and ball games dominated the play space with a few swings and teeter–totters towards the front edge. One May Day, we girls tried to weave ribbons, dancing around a maypole, and ended up with such a tangle that Teacher almost cried in embarrassment. Not until I went to a city school did I encounter physically rougher contests like Red Rover and King of the Hill, which was just as well.

When weather meant recess indoors, we played musical chairs or our teacher read to us from Thornton Burgess or others of his ilk. My favorites were the Uncle Wiggily stories, widely syndicated in newspapers, and reprinted in books.

The author, Howard R. Garis, was born at 18 Doubleday Street in Binghamton. In 1910, he created his first Uncle Wiggily as a special assignment, in addition to covering the police beat for a New Jersey daily newspaper. Edward M. Scudder, who owned and published the *Newark News*, decided to print a child's story every day, and Garis wrote six 700–word chapters weekly for over 50 years. No wonder the Uncle Wiggily board game, invented in 1917, became the best–selling game for children in the world.

My beat–up copy of *Uncle Wiggily's Airship* delights me still, particularly the suspense–filled promises ending every chapter. Here are a few:

". . . in the story after this, if the rose bush doesn't scratch the eyes out of the potato salad, I'll tell you about. . . "

". . . if the blackbird on our fence doesn't pick all the clothes pins off the chocolate cake . . ."

". . . if my typewriter doesn't go in swimming and get its hair ribbon all wet, so it's as crinkly as a corkscrew . . ."

". . . if the lemonade pitcher doesn't go to the ink well for a glass of jelly . . ."

". . . if the tomato doesn't jump out of the coffee can, and kiss the cucumber salad in the olive oil, I'll tell you next about Uncle Wiggily and the lemonade stand."

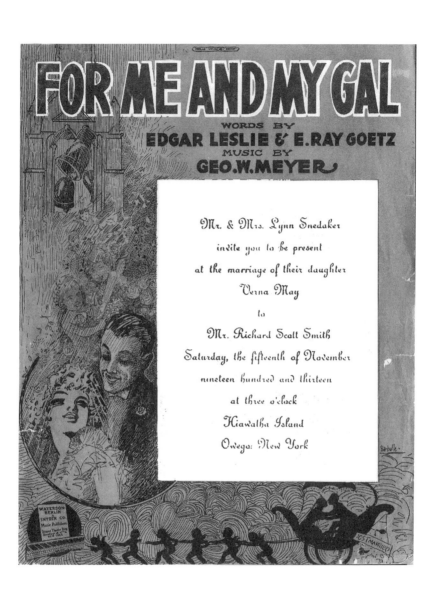

FOR ME AND MY GAL

WORDS BY
EDGAR LESLIE & E. RAY GOETZ
MUSIC BY
GEO. W. MEYER

Mr. & Mrs. Lynn Snedaker
invite you to be present
at the marriage of their daughter
Verna May
to
Mr. Richard Scott Smith
Saturday, the fifteenth of November
nineteen hundred and thirteen
at three o'clock
Hiawatha Island
Owego: New York

CHAPTER 6

Vignettes of Verna

My memories of ferry house days are more accurately of family stories. We lived there only one year. Dad prepared a small garden plot and Mother took over. Peas are planted while patches of snow still show, lettuce and radishes soon after, corn, beans, and potatoes as the soil warms. Before they were ready, wild edibles abounded as greens. The slightly bitter bite of pre–bud dandelions led the parade, followed by tender sprouts of milkweed, small whorls of wild mustard, and what we called pigweed — green amaranth.

Dora, daughter of Mandy and Sid Groesbeck, was a generation closer to Rensselaer Barton than I. They lived nearby. Dora awed me with her artistic ability. Their china closet was resplendent with sugar bowls, creamers, and china plates she had hand–painted with rose garlands. Later, she taught me my first piano scales. She told me of when she was little and her grandfather occasionally let her start the engine and run the ferry.

Rance was a wagon builder, cabinet maker, and resident of Owego until he took up a homestead claim in Minnesota. By the time Amanda Melvina, his thirteenth and last child, was seven, her education became a matter of greater importance than the economics of continuing through more harsh winters and difficult growing seasons encountered in that school–less territory. Her mother, Effie Ann, Rance's second wife, had taught her at the kitchen table.

So, they returned to Owego in about 1870 and Rance bought the wagon boat ferry that crossed the river about a quarter of a mile above Hiawatha Island. He proceeded to modernize it.

He built a second boat to house a steam boiler and he himself forged a heavy chain which reached across the river. Some of its links hang today in the Tioga County Historical Museum on Front Street in Owego. The chain passed around two large cogged wheels whose axles were the connection between the two boats. The ferry was driven by a steam engine. For greater stability, the boats were guyed by four wires to two cables which acted to minimize sway.

After Owego Free Academy closed for the 1911 summer vacation, Verna tended me, more or less. As a crawler, I was already Mother's little runaway, still in the walk–and–tumble stage. The lane beckoned me . . . all uphill, past the meadow, over double railroad tracks, beyond further fields to the main road. I might have made it but for the brindle cow who put her head between the fence bars and mooed a mighty inquiry. Mother scooped me into her arms as I retreated, bawling.

☆ ☆ ☆

Both parents were busy. They put a couple of planks from the bank to the apron of the ferry and another piece leading into the engine house. Tumbling ice cluttered the river, which was still too high for shore landing. Wind buffeted the ferry about as they fired up the boiler for a trial.

Verna was sternly admonished to keep her eye on me. She became engrossed in a novel and never noticed my wandering off until Father, fierce in his anger, loomed beside her. I had walked the plank on uncertain baby legs and grabbed at Mother's skirts. Neither of them heard me above the coughing and hissing of the boiler and engine and the swishing and clunking of the elements. My guardian angel earned a special star that day.

Verna's sparkling eyes were the color and liveliness of woods violets tossing in a gentle breeze and her hair was a soft brown, like the velvet fur of small mice. She was ever the blithe spirit. How else can I account for remembrances from when she was engaged?

From an original oil painting by Verna Snedaker Smith. The Barton Ferry Landing on the north shore of the Susquehanna River.

She and Scott Smith married just after my third birthday.

Both she and mother played the piano. Mom's favorite song foretold the age of radio — *"There's Music in the Air."* Verna sang, *"I Dreamt That I Dwelt in Marble Halls"* from Balfe's *Bohemian Girl.* I was only two feathers weightier than a sparrow, so Verna clasped me under my arms and waltzed me about the room, gazing into my eyes. I dreamt along with her, saw the vassals and serfs in attendance, suitors arriving, knights on bended knee pledging their faith. "And this is the best part of all, Eupha Mae." She sang in her lovely girlish voice, "I dreamt that one of that noble band came forth my hand to claim, but I also dreamt, which pleased me most, that Scott loved me still the same. He loves me, Eupha. We are engaged! This winter, we are going to be married!"

Verna was happy to be engaged so I was happy for her. It was all ever so romantic — until I overheard someone ask if she had enough sheets and pillow cases in her hope chest for their new bedroom at the Smith Farm.

Horrors! My beloved sister was going to move away and leave me!

I was crushed. I went to my room and buried my head in a pillow. Nobody knew or cared. Everyone else was merry. Why would Mamma and Papa help her leave us if they really loved her? My joy had flown. I moped about the house for two or three days before anyone noticed. The place was a beehive of activity.

Verna called Carl and me to her bedroom the evening before the wedding. She reached out to hug me, but I held back, betrayed. She dropped her hand and spoke in a low voice. "Tomorrow, lots of people are coming for the wedding. I want you to be just as happy as Scott and I are." Verna smiled straight at me. "You aren't losing me. I will always be your sister, even when we're old and gray." I tittered at such an improbable notion. "You're gaining a brother–in–law, like a big brother for both of you."

I wasn't sure I wanted another brother like Carl. I drew a deep breath. No, Scott wouldn't become another Carl. He'd always be Scott, laughing, joking, teasing me in a good–natured way. (It was Carl who changed, along with me, as we matured.)

"But Verna, you won't live here anymore. I won't put your plate on the table when we get ready to eat." Tears brimmed again.

"We'll both come back often and eat with you. And you'll come over to the mainland and eat with us. We'll lunch together, Eupha, you and I."

"At night, you'll stay there and I'll come back without you."

"Not always. You can stay overnight sometimes!"

"And eat breakfast with you, too?"

". . . Breakfast too, you little goose. Now dry your eyes. We don't want them looking like a couple of red potatoes tomorrow. When I promise to love, honor, and obey, and Scott lifts my long veil and kisses me, you'll laugh and clap and cheer with everyone!"

That next day, our seldom–used parlor was open and filled with chairs for guests. They came in droves, by train, carriage, and car, from Owego, Newark Valley, Binghamton, Whitney Point, Hamilton Vestal Center, Union and Lestershire (later re–named Endicott and Johnson City, for the "E"and "J" in E–J Shoes), and Athens, at the Pennsylvania state line. Ferry and row boats crossed time and again, augmented by the boats of our Hiawatha and Apalachin neighbors once their wives and children had stepped ashore.

Verna and Scott plighted their troth beneath a bough–and–ground–pine–festooned arch way. A great golden yellow crepe paper wedding bell hung over their heads. I was sure cupids flew about unseen. I wondered why some women cried when the knot was tied. I certainly didn't!

Never had Mom's cut glass gleamed so brightly nor her silver-ware been polished to such brilliance. The meal was sumptuous enough to last the whole day, for guests faced lengthy return trips. Never had Hiawatha Island witnessed such a wedding!

Verna slipped away to change from her floor–sweeping ivory satin gown into a suit for their honeymoon trip. Amid much josh-ing and well–wishing, the two ran hand–in–hand to the landing.

Not a boat was to be found.!

A Hiawatha Island Childhood 1911 – 1919

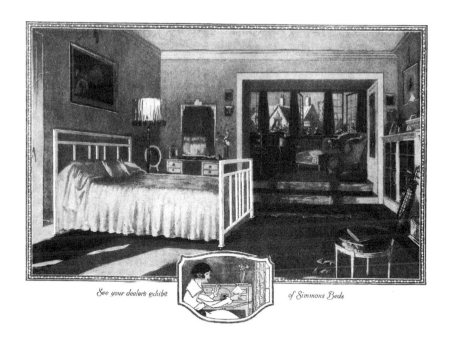

CHAPTER 7

Suzie's Room

Verna remained my idol among young women. On those halcy-on days spent at her place, I peeked into the lives and habits of other slightly older ones, Scott's sisters, and remained a bit in awe of all but Suzie.

The Rev. Richard Smith, Methodist, retired, ran a large farm assisted by Scott and Arthur, his younger sons. IBM–Owego even-tually took over where the pleasant big farmhouse stood back from Day Hollow Road. Its umpteen rooms and wings were spacious, its kitchen cavernous. I loved a strange narrow circular staircase off the kitchen. Sensible oldsters avoided its wedge–shaped, toe–sized treads. My feet fit.

A private porch on Scott and Verna's wing faced a different direc-tion from the main one which wrapped around the corner of the for-

The Oliver Typewriter Co
No. 9

mal parlor and music room. Just beyond the door which led from their part into the main house was another staircase with a small study Scott's father seldom used, just off the landing. That kind man let me play away at his Oliver typewriter, even sliding fresh paper into it for me. Impressions were faint, the ribbon being quite dry. The Oliver was designed so no casing hid its banked–type keys. Hunting and pecking, I watched every movement.

Upstairs bedrooms, their windows open to every breeze that stirred on the brow of the hill, came as close to summer air conditioning as we then knew.

Suzie's room was my favorite. She made me welcome when there and left word it was okay for me to be there when she wasn't. Grass rugs on polished wooden floors and wicker chairs with cretonne cushions invited me to sit and sense serenity. A slant–front lid on her small desk was usually open for writing letters and there she kept her white shaggy–coated and ink–spotted toy dog. She wiped her pens on him!

"Oh, my goodness," I thought, "she's spoiling him!"

She laughed. "He's different this week than last. A leopard can't change his spots, but Mopsy adds to his!" Some blobs were almost coppery from the pressure of replacing a worn nib in those pre–fountain-pen days.

Suzie had long summer vacations. She taught in private girls' schools. I had no desire to attend one.

A strict monitor inspects every night before lights out. Clothes must be folded neatly on each bedside chair, shoes placed toe–to–toe, heel–to–heel, just under the edge of the bed. If not, the monitor pulls

a girl out of bed, and watches every move. She
doesn't say a word. Just watches like a hawk.

Students learned French or German to the point of fluency.
Mary Janeth was a wee tyke when Suzie taught her all the verses of
Silent Night in German. At the next Hiawatha Club meeting, Suzie
announced with some fanfare that her niece would honor them
with her first solo. "With my aunt nodding encouragement from
the piano, the Christmas season was launched, " Mary Jan recalls.

Children loved Suzie who was not much bigger than they.
Adults enjoyed her good–natured humor. She eventually retired to
Florida and married for the first time. Jan tells of arriving at their
beach house to find Suzie rubbing her knees.

"Rheumatism getting you, Aunt Suzie?"

"Heavens no. I fell off my bicycle!"

She was then past seventy.

Icy Smith was the sedate sister. When I first learned she worked
at the school, but wasn't a teacher, I discovered what secretaries
do. Icy was in the Owego system as secretary to the superintendent
until her retirement. She never married. She had planned to, but
one crisp winter's evening when stars sparkled and the pond invited, she and her fiancé went skating. They both broke through the
thin ice. He drowned. She was buoyed by air trapped in her
leg–o–mutton sleeves. He was the one man on earth for her. She
knew there was no other.

Icy cared about other people's children. She was always neat and
business–like. I recall her in a crisp white shirtwaist and long
worsted skirt, with a sweater at hand.

Scott's oldest, red–haried sister, Dr. Mary White, practiced
medicine with her husband, Dr. Ben, in Bradford, Pennsylvania
and came back only infrequently. I happened to be at the Smith's
once as the couple prepared to leave in an early morning fog.

"My hair! This weather makes it all stringy!" she moaned.

Dr. Mary did a man's work in her practice, but womanly
instincts persisted.

A Hiawatha Island Childhood 1911 – 1919

CHAPTER 8

Geometrically Cued

At a time when most of my friends were having headaches over it, I found geometry a bowl of cherries. Unbeknown to either of us at the time, Dad had cued me into math before I was five.

Charles Marvin, who owned the island, was a well–to–do retiree with aspirations toward being a gentlemen farmer. He wanted to try some agrarian experiments such as raising turkeys and growing alfalfa, so he hired my father to do the hands–on management.

Dad was a good choice, experienced in more than just raising crops, kindly and temperate in his ways, and aware of a problem when he encountered one.

According to the deed, the island was "One hundred acres, more or less." How could it be more definite? Do you calculate from the high–water mark? Then what about the cutbank on the south shore, which in any spring break–up could change its contours?

Most of the farm was arable. We never, except for Christmas, cut healthy trees from the section too big to be called a grove. To us, it was "the woods." The punchbowl was left to native grasses. No matter how heavy a rain, water never accumulated in the bowl. Occasional shards of pottery, pieces of flint, and other evidence of long–ago Seneca campfires emerged there.

My brother rode the school wagon, or sleigh in snow–time, to Owego. This was not rapid transit and left very little daylight, either morning or night, for Carl to help with chores. In fact, for several weeks each year he boarded in town while the river ran slush too thick to row, or formed thin ice which would support only squirrels and rabbits. The farm was too big for one man to handle alone. We needed help to live with us as part of the family.

Not every husky lad was willing to hire out to a farm with little possibility of getting to town on payday. Rest and recreation was not part of the general vocabulary, but it entered into Dad's thinking.

So, one memorable day, the freight office phoned and Dad hitched his strongest team to the lumber wagon, ferried to the mainland, and drove to the station. Everyone involved in getting the shipment loaded or unloaded agreed that it weighed a ton! Naturally, since it was a full–sized. slate–topped, factory–crated Brunswick pool table!

I was banished from the house while the men maneuvered it through two stair landings into the extra–large upstairs room. When I got back inside, Dad was busy replacing handrails and newel posts. I dashed past him for my first sight.

Oh, it was beautiful! It boasted massive square walnut legs with ornamental ball turnings and glossy varnish, with raised and cushioned edges. The top surface was inlaid in mother–of–pearl. The heavy cord–netted pockets were the same inspiring green as the baize on which a triangular frame held 15 balls. Each was different. Glossy balls of magenta, orange, blue, etc., each had a number in a white spot. White balls were color–banded around the number. An oak wall rack held five long tapered cues with octagonal handholds at the thicker end and perfect little padded leather tips which needed frequent powdering with a cube of green chalk to keep them from glancing off the ball. An arched bridge with a long handle was a gizmo to steady a shot made from near the middle of the five–by–ten foot table.

Dad spent a lot of time getting it exactly oriented, placing his long carpenter's level lengthwise, then crosswise, as he adjusted height with built–in disk screws. Then he made a diminutive scaled–down cue stick, just for me! Mother papered the wall with colored covers from farm magazines and *The Saturday Evening Post*, and I grew up with Norman Rockwell art.

That room served as bait to attract the best, the strongest, and the most willing young men. Dad wouldn't allow smoking, boozing, or any curse stronger than a "darn," so over the years we had a succession of the county's finest, every one my friend. The only names I still remember are Ralph Van Atta and Walter Cheeseman. It's been 75 years, for goodness sake!

Dad taught me to climb onto a tall stool in the corner to watch and learn. Someone would say, "There, it's Eupha Mae's turn." I'd jump down and squeal, "Hold me up! I want to get that three spot!" or whatever. A grinning hired man upsie–daisied me since I was far too small to reach over the edge.

For the target ball to roll straight, the cue ball must hit it dead center. A bit to the right or left causes the ball to ricochet (how I loved sound of that word!) off the padded sides. It's easy to forget that the cue ball changed directions, too. If it lands in a pocket, you're penalized. Sometimes the best shot aims at the edge first. It's all a science of angles. Surprisingly, I was soon scoring quite a few balls. Not surprisingly, Snedaker's hired men had the reputation of being almost unbeatable when they did get to the pool hall in Owego.

I must have been five or six years old when Mother went to Virginia to visit two nieces who had lived with our family while in nurses' training before I was born. She planned to take me, but infantile paralysis was on the rampage. The final week before she left, Dad arranged for his aged aunt to come and I stayed home with her. Mother closed and locked the door to the room with the pool table and admonished the men to do something else that week. Aunt Mary had her own ideas of what was proper, it seemed.

She arrived on the same train that Mother left on. Stowing her wraps properly in the closet, she took me on her lap. "Let's get acquainted, Eupha Mae. Do you like to play house?"

"Oh, yes. I love my dolls and I have a whole great big box of paper ones, too."

"Do you like to hear stories?"

"Oh yes, and I like to read them, too!"

"You can read? Why, Eupha Mae, that's wonderful! After supper we'll turn up the lamp and you can read to me."

"Oh no. After supper, I want to play pool."

She drew back, shocked. But then, she hugged me, chuckling at what she presumed was a childish confusion of phrase for heaven–knows–what.

During her stay, after the supper dishes were done, the range reservoir refilled, and the double boiler of oat flakes left to simmer all night on the back of the stove, we had story hour until bedtime. The hired man sulked in the kitchen and ate all the cookies.

The summer my youngest brother was born, we left the island and never again had a good place for the pool table. When it went into the attic in Binghamton, Dad pronounced it "the last time I'll ever hassle with that unwieldy beast," and it may still be there where it's too hot and dusty in the summer and too chilly and drafty the rest of the time. We didn't miss it much after we discovered 15–cent movies in the neighborhood.

Snow–blessed winters of sledding and skating merged into lilac–scented springs and garden plantings, summer vacations, autumns of maple glory and the return to classes. The day I opened my Euclid to a series of "abc" and "xyz" diagrams, my thoughts ricocheted to a fun–filled room with an always willing youth a dozen years my senior to hoist me up for an "eight ball in

the right side pocket." Yes, geometry would be duck soup for me.
I never stopped with the homework assignment. By the end of the
year, I'd done every probelm in the book., just for enjoyment..

My by then deceased Great Aunt Mary would have been —
well — flabbergasted!

A Special Grace

Mom found it in a weedy place,
She put it in her green–glass vase
And smiling, called it
"Queen Anne's Lace."

When someone asked, "Why gather weeds?"
She gently answered, "Souls have needs
And on such beauty
My soul feeds."

Eupha M. Shanly

CHAPTER 9

I Remember Mamma's Baking

"Mother, what does layser mean?"

"I'm not sure. How is it used?"

I read from my storybook: "It would seem, Frank declared, that Ralph has too much layser time."

Mom chuckled, but didn't stop the steady push and pound of her bread kneading. "And how do you spell it?"

"L–E–I . . . but it's not "I before C," so it has to be sounded like A — as–in–neighbor–and–weigh . . . S–U–R–E."

"It's a funny spelling, Eupha Mae, but it's pronounced lee–zhur, and it means that Ralph isn't working. They say the Devil finds work for idle hands to do."

I decided then and there that leisure must be a form of laziness and was glad the Devil didn't need to come to the Island. We always found plenty of work without his assistance, honest and enjoyable work, not drudgery such as some associate with farming. I heard of a man who didn't know, when he was doing chores, that he was learning how to farm. "I thought I was being punished."

Like the United States, my mother was *e pluribus unum*, "one out of many" good cooks in the area. She baked bread once or twice a week, using an unusual bread–making machine, a huge covered bowl with top crank connected to paddles which worked the dough very well. Each batch made enough for four to six loaves. She removed the large bread board from its slide–in place in the Hoosier kitchen cabinet, put it on the cabinet's white enameled work surface and floured it well. With greased bread pans ready and at hand, she dumped the dough and cut it with a knife into pie-shaped chunks, then formed them into individual loaves. Even though her hands were amply floured, her fingers became webbed with dough at this stage, no time for the telephone to ring! She couldn't answer until the loaves were panned, covered with clean towels to avoid drafts, and left to rise.

How fast they rose depended on the weather. Usually each was punched down and left for a second rising, for better textured bread, free of big air holes. Often she used the waiting time to make cookies, bake macaroni and cheese or beans, or perhaps a pie or two. A thermometer in the door of the range oven would have been helpful, but she could judge accurately by sticking her hand into the oven.

Our orchard yielded a variety of apples from early summer on. Some were crunchy and juicy to eat out–of–hand, others were pie timber, or the makings for Mom's yummy apple dumplings. Here's how she went about creating those pre–tastes of paradise.

Put into the top of a large size double boiler, two cups each of water and sugar, a couple of tablespoons of butter, a teaspoon of cinnamon and 1/4 teaspoon of nutmeg. Sometimes she added cloves. It took about five minutes for the sugar to dissolve completely and boil.

To keep the syrup warm without getting too thick, she set it into the double boiler base pushed to the back of the stove and turned to making a rich dough from two and a half cups of flour, two teaspoons Royal baking powder, and 3/4 teaspoons of salt, sifted together. With two knives, she cut in a half cup of shortening, which usually meant lard from the last butchering. When it

reached the "fine as corn meal" stage, she added about 3/4 cup milk, in driblets, to make a soft yet not runny dough.

This was kneaded a few times, then patted out to a quarter–inch thickness and cut into half a dozen squares. A good pile of sliced apples, with some sugar and cinnamon and a dab of butter, went onto each square. Then the corners were pulled up and pinched together. She'd wet her fingers and scallop-pinch along the seams too. Then they went, upside down, into a greased baking pan. She poured the hot syrup to cover them and cut A–for-apple-shaped slits into the top of each so they wouldn't explode from the build–up of steam. They started in a hot oven, probably around 425 degrees, for ten minutes. Then she slipped pans of cool water into the oven to lower the heat by 50 degrees and baked them for another half–hour or so. Served warm with their own syrup, they were mouth–watering. Some of the family poured rich milk on top, but to me that was just gilding the lily.

Kitchen Necessities

A food chopper, fruit press, baking pan, two–lipped rounded–bottom saucepan, an iron dutch oven, wooden bowl and spoon, and large and small baking dishes are utensils every woman should have.

From the March 1917 issue of
The Ladies Home Journal

CHAPTER 10

Riddle – Me – Ree

I stood on a kitchen chair by the table watching Mother sift flour and baking powder for a cake. She cracked an egg over a bowl, poured all of it into a half-shell, letting the white go into a bowl. Then she tipped the rest very slowly into the other half-shell to separate the yolk into a second small bowl. She always did this to make sure the egg was fresh, and usually beat up the bowls separately "to make the cake lighter." She reached for the second egg.

"Here's a riddle for you." she said.

> In marble walls as white as milk,
> Lined with a skin as soft as silk,
> Within a fountain crystal clear,
> A golden apple doth appear.
> No doors there are to this stronghold,
> Yet thieves break in and steal the gold.

"What is it?"

My forehead wrinkled. I was thinking, but mostly about that "fountain crystal clear." The only fountain I knew was the Fireman's Memorial on courthouse square in Owego, which all summer bubbled water up and over the edge.

"Say it again."

Mother recited it, pausing often to let me consider what she was saying. Still baffled, I shook my head.

Mother smiled and said, "Now, watch me while I repeat it again." She reached for the third egg, glancing back and forth between me and the bowls. As she slipped the yolk from the shell, she was smiling. "A golden apple doth appear."

"It's an egg!" I shouted, clapping my hands. "I like that even better than Humpty Dumpty's getting broken."

Dad was a great one, too, for riddles and stories. One evening, he asked me how I was doing in arithmetic. I grunted. Arithmetic was not my favorite subject.

"See if you can figure this out. As I was going to St. Ives, I met a man with seven wives; every wife had seven sacks and every sack had seven cats. Every cat had seven kits. Kits, cats, sacks,. and wives! How many were going to St. Ives?"

"That's too hard," I protested. "Seven times seven is 49, but then it's seven times that, and seven times that again, and adding them all . . . It's too hard."

"Not if you think it out. Where was I going?"

"To St. Ives . . . Where's that?"

"In England. And I met a man with all those wives. Where were they going?"

"I don't know. Maybe they were coming from St. Ives."

"Exactly." Dad laughed, and I with him. That was a good one. I memorized it to try out on some of the kids on the school wagon.

Then there was the one starting, "Riddle–me, riddle–me, rid-dle–me–ree, perhaps you can tell what this riddle may be. As deep as a house, as round as a cup. And all the King's horses can't draw it up!"

It seems to me that what with this and Humpty Dumpty, the king's horses must be getting tired. We didn't have an open well on the island, but I'd seen them in other yards, and even hollered down one that had a bucket to pull up. With a few hints, I got that one, too.

> Elizabeth, Lizzy, Betsy, and Bess,
> All went together to seek a bird's nest.
> They found a nest with five eggs in it.
> They each took one, and left four in it.

That got me interested in nicknames. I knew a Libby and a Betty. They obviously came from Elizabeth, too.

"What's Aunt Kit's real name?"

"Katherine. Kate is another short form. What do you think Aunt

Gerty was named when she was born?"

"I don't know."

"Well, think." A long silence.

"Is it Gertrude?"

"Yes. I doubt you know Aunt Tennie's name. It's Hortense. Aunt Mandy is Amanda. Aunt Fan is Fannie. Aunt Nell may be Eleanor."

"Aren't any of my Aunts called by their real names?"

"Yes. Lena, Jess, Vera, Hazel, and Helen."

Mother's name was Mertie, named for an aunt on her mother's side who may have been named for somebody named Myrtle for all we know.

When I asked Dad about his brothers, I was surprised. Uncle Gene was Eugene, Uncle Lias was Elias, Uncle John was Jonathan. Uncle Jim was James Malone, Uncle Joe was Joseph. Lee, who died as a boy, was named for the Civil War general.

"But you are really Lynn, aren't you?" I pleaded. I couldn't imagine my daddy not using his right name.

"Well, when I was born, births weren't registered. Now, anybody can look up your birth certificate at the Broome County registrar's office in Binghamton. I've been told that my father, Cornelius, wanted Alinzer and Mother didn't argue about it. She just started calling me Lynn from the day I was born. When I registered to vote, I put down Lynn W. Snedaker, without a qualm."

"What does the W stand for?"

"Absolutely nothing. When I lived in Morristown, I got mail that came from nobody I knew. Turned out there was another Lynn Snedaker and he was older than I. I sat down and wrote Lynn A., Lynn B., Lynn C., etc., and when I came to the W, that was it. So I let everybody know and started to get just the mail I was meant to," he chuckled.

One more riddle. We used kerosene lamps and lanterns, but my folks grew up with candles.

> Little Nancy Etticoat in a white petticoat
> And a red nose.
> The longer she stands, the shorter she grows.

WHO HAS SEEN THE WIND?

Who has seen the wind?
　Neither I or you:
But when the leaves hang trembling,
　The wind is passing through.

Who has seen the wind?
　Neither you nor I:
But when the trees bow down their heads
　The wind is passing by.

CHRISTINA GEORGINA ROSSETTI.

CHAPTER 11

A Bang – Up Blow

This washday went well, with bright sun and a light drying breeze. Mother stood sorting the last basketful from the clothes line. One pile needed sprinkling for tomorrow's ironing. The rest she folded, smoothing out hems and small wrinkles with her hands. Some folks slept on ironed sheets. We Snedakers smelled the ozone of fresh ones.

A distant rumble of thunder alerted Mother. "Eupha Mae, go through the front door and get those towels and white shirts we've been bleaching on the lawn grass."

My obstinate streak was showing. "They aren't dry, Mamma. I felt them a few minutes ago."

"Well, they won't get any drier from the sound of things. Run along."

She herself dashed off to the chicken yard to make certain all the biddies went up their slant walk into the hennery. Those leghorns and Rhode Island reds provided many Sunday dinners, all the eggs we could eat, and egg money besides. She flapped her apron to get the last of the hens inside, slid a plank in place closing the entrance, and then braced the big door. She didn't trust the latch to hold if it gusted. On the way back, she detoured to throw the circuit breaker on the side of the house, by the golden glows. Lightning rods couldn't protect against a bolt following open telephone wires.

Dad raced the team to get them into the barn before the fast–approaching storm hit. Mother waved at him. He stayed with his horses to unharness and rub them down. By that time, big drops pockmarked the dust in the lane.

He didn't need to worry about the cows. They'd turn their back-sides to the wind and drift before it, finding a low spot or the lee of a rise to head in close together.

Mother hurried upstairs. The bathroom and bedroom windows were all open. Their soaking wet white voile curtains slapped her face and wrapped around her arms as she struggled to pull the screens out and slam down the lower sashes. She had to get bath towels to sop up puddles from the varnished floors, and dry the painted window sills. She changed into a fresh crisp house dress before coming back downstairs.

Meanwhile, I'd drawn a kitchen chair to the window beyond the range and rested on my knees, peering out. I loved the drama of a good storm — the sounds, the lightning flashes, the whipping branches, but this was no ordinary stage show. Things were crash-ing. Something slammed against the side of the shed. The wind whistled with such ferocity that it drove heavy rain in horizontal streaks. I couldn't see a thing there, so I climbed down and ran to the back door. Powerful gusts pushed against it, which made me all the more determined to open it. I did and somehow got outside. Wham! The door slammed shut with part of my skirt caught inside.

Wind–driven raindrops were like needles piercing my skin. My thin dress was saturated, my wet hair was streaming, and I was screaming and fighting to get back where I belonged. Mother couldn't have heard me above the racket, but she saw a triangle of skirt and rescued me. I was shaking uncontrollably, in shock.

She wasted no time in words. Stripping off my clothes, she wound me tightly in a still sun–warmed sheet, like a cocoon. The swaddling quieted my trembling. Then she stood back, crossed her arms, and studied me.

She chuckled. "Your hair needs washing, so why don't we finish the job?"

She filled a big bowl from the stove's reservoir of hot water, gave me a folded face cloth to keep the soap out of my eyes, and worked up a fine Ivory Soap lather. Two plain rinses, a cider vine-gar rise, and a brisk toweling followed. She folded, wrapped, and pinned a large bath towel like a turban, then carried me to my bed and slipped a hot water bottle near my feet.

"There." she said. "That'll help dry your hair."

Exhaustion took over. I was asleep in seconds.

The next morning, as my parents assessed the damage and started fixing things up, I explored mud puddles. In the half-drowned garden, among beaten–down muddy leaves, I found a huge ripe cucumber, completely yellowed, its skin as tough as saddle leather. At noon, Mother got out her sharpest butcher knife to cut it in half lengthwise, and gave me a metal tablespoon.

I scooped out most of the pulp, dumped that into the swill pail, and spent the remainder of the day maneuvering two saffron boats in deep sea puddles. Never did master the trick of keeping triangular cut–paper sails upright but I swished about barefoot and got gloriously muddy trying to.

The Ladies of The Hiawatha Club, 1914–15. An incomplete list of members through the years, compiled from news items includes: Mrs. James A. Archibald (Anna), Mrs. George Bodle (Georgia) #6, Mrs. D.M. Curran, Susie Curran #30, Mrs. Dennis, Mrs. DeWitt DeGroat, Mrs. Goodsell A. Ford (Matie) #16?, Mrs. Gaskill (Norman's mother), Mrs. Edward E. Griffen, Mrs. Theodore (Amanda) Groesbeck #19, her daughter, Dora Groesbeck (later Mrs. Walter Partridge), Mrs. John Groesbeck (Adelaide), , Mrs. Richard T. Hodge, Mrs. Hunt, Mrs. B.B. Hughes, Mrs. Ingersoll, Mrs. Johnson, Mrs. C.V. Jones, Mrs. LaMonte, from Owego, Mrs. G.B. Mead, Mrs. Homer C. Mead (Mary Jones) #12, Mrs. D.M. Meade, Mrs. Cecelia Patterson (later Mrs. Ira Buck of Pittsburgh), Mrs. Leona Paetzold, Mrs. Mertie Rising (Olive's mother), Vesta Robinson (Riker's mother), Mrs. Harry W. Rowe #27?, Mildred Shiek (or Scheik), Mrs. Richard J. (Harriet) Smith #1, Sue Smith, Mrs. Arthur H. Smith (Maysie) #10, Mrs. Scott Smith (Verna) #3, Mrs. Lynn W. Snedaker (Mertie) #18, Mrs. Judson Spencer (Marion) #29?, Mrs. Harry Tilbury (Mary), Mrs. VanHousen, Mrs. A.W. Waldron, Mrs. Westerner, Mrs. Frank White, Mrs. Zimmer (Ralph's mother).

The author, Eupha Mae Snedaker, is #2

CHAPTER 12

The Hiawatha Club

The Hiawatha Club took over the schoolhouse when the district consolidated with Owego. It looms high in my mountain of memories. The women's study group was instigated in 1904 by Mrs. Richard J. Smith, Mrs. George Bodle, Mrs. Mary Tilbury, Mrs. Theodore Groesbeck — my Great Aunt Mandy, and several others. In 1917–18, they met weekly to do Red Cross work for the American Red Cross. Until then, they concentrated on American History and Literature.

In 1916, the year Verna's baby, Mary Janeth, was born, Mother was president. She hand–printed the program book. It was about four inches square. The green cover was of oatmeal–textured wall paper, attached with yarn tied through punched holes. At the end of her term, the ladies gave her an appreciation gift, a soft, suede leather–bound copy of Whittier's Poems, which I came to love as bedtime read–to–me's. So, for my twelfth Christmas, Verna gave me the Whittier Birthday Book with a quotation for every day.

I was at the meeting when Mother recited a verse she'd found about the daily sacrifices imposed on Americans in order to help a besieged Europe. "Our Mondays are wheatless, our Tuesdays are meatless. On Wednesdays we go without . . . " leading to the final, "Oh God, how I hate the Kaiser." If only I could have located that piece of paper! It's not in her scrapbook. The members exchanged a lot of hints and recipes for coping.

Mrs. B.B. Hughes arranged for a program of illustrated songs and nursery rhymes for the November meeting. She asked me to be Little Miss Muffet who sat on a tuffet and she promised me a gift as a reward for my cooperation.

For this, my first stage appearance, Mother costumed me with a

purple lace–edged mob cap, a white voile shawl collar worn over my best winter dress and a pretty overskirt puffed at the hips. Seated on a stool, I pantomimed eating a bowlful of curds and whey from a table which was really our own mahogany piano stool that had glass ball feet and a seat that spiral-adjusted from high to low. Brown and green horse blankets were suspended on three sides from ceiling wires to suggest a small room.

Verna stood on a high stool behind the blankets and dangled a big, black woolly spider in front of my face. I was startled! I threw my arms above my head and the spoon clattered to the floor as I ran around to my sister. The ladies were all clapping.

"You did just fine," she told me proudly.

My gift? The ugly black toy spider! I carried him in my pocket and produced him at odd times, hoping to scare someone. I never did, though. He was too gargantuan to be taken for real. However, just one of his hairy legs sticking out from a bowl of fruit — that got attention.

The evening ended with Suzie, Verna's vivacious sister–in–law, reading her original poem, a take–off on members and their families. She called it, "The Fly on the Wall." and that WAS pasted in Mom's scrapbook.

CHAPTER 13

The Fly on the Wall

It was cold Thanksgiving weather,
Not so many years ago,
When the small white country schoolhouse
Was with bright lights all aglow.

How I got there, 'tis a marvel,
For my fly friends long ago
Had flown away to warmer regions
Or died 'neath flakes of snow.

But the old wood stove was blazing,
And woke me from my sleep
Upon the long, black stovepipe.
I just had to take one peep.

And when the smoke came up the chimney
And the pipe became so hot,
I flew up on the ceiling
Lest I get an "awful swat."

For Addie Groesbeck was to be there,
And she kills every poor house–fly
That ever ventures in her home,
And I didn't want to die.

It seems the knowledge factory
Was soon to see a merry sight,
For the "Hiawatha Club" was coming
There — to dine, that Winter night.

One by one, they slowly gathered,
From the valley and the hill;
The Fords blew in from Broadway,
Each was there to get his fill.

LaMontes from town soon joined the party
Gaskill Corners sent some, too,
Johnsons came across the river
In their ice–boat, painted blue.

In pranced Mrs. DeGroat in a flurry,
Out of breath, she's hurried so,
But she smiled and simply stated,
I'd been here sooner but DeWitt's so slow!

The Currans put in appearance,
Mother, Father, don't they look fine?
"Baby Sue" and "Uncle Schuyler,"
'Cause they couldn't leave them behind.

Schuyler and Father carried the boxes,
Veal loaves for the ladies and gents;
Loaves made by the new meat chopper
That was bought for eighty cents.

The Snedakers came with bag and baggage,
Including Eupha Mae.
They had crossed the ice together
On this cold Thanksgiving Day.

Even to a fly it was exciting,
I did so want to buzz
When I saw the eats Lynn carried
'Neath his coat of fur and fuzz.

Then I thought an earthquake coming,
Such a jangle of sounds and tone,
Both school doors flew open together,
To let in the noisy Smiths and Jones.

Then in walked little Mrs. Zimmer;
Eugene and Ralph, too, were there.
Father carried a market basket
Containing the Zimmer son and heir.

Then Mrs. Gaskill and her husband,
He at a rather rapid pace
With a smile of anticipation
On his broad and jovial face.

Such salads and such frosted cakes
That the Spencers and Tilburys brought
Such candies and other "goodies"
O'er which Frances and Eunice fought.

The Shieks blew in together,
A noisy, happy bunch,
The breezy Westerners were there with them,
And some more good–looking lunch.

Oh! To roost one tiny minute
On that delicious spicy food.
I wanted some so badly,
But I couldn't be so rude.

So I waited until the VanHousens
And the Hunts had all arrived:
Then the Masons and Mrs. VanAtta
With Frances clinging to her side.

Oh! The aroma of the coffee!
Oh! The sip from the coffee cup!
I wished — then dozed for a few seconds
When a crash woke me up!

G.B. Mead and Uncle Schuyler,
Lynn Snedaker, too — the crazy "boobs" —
Had been sitting on a bench together,
When it broke and let down the "rubes!"

How "Sid" Groesbeck laughed to see them!
Seemed to tickle Bodle, too,
For he chuckled and said so quickly,
"Wonder you didn't go right through."

When the crowd had finished eating
All the turkey and the pie,
I knew they would leave some crumbs for me,
So I winked the other eye.

And waited until they arose to sing,
"My Country 'Tis of Thee,"
Makes a fly feel good to think he lives
In the home of the brave and the free.

The crowd all sang so lustily
The patriotic refrain.
Sue Curran pumped the old school organ
With all her might and main.

Soon the guests had all departed
In fur robe, coat, and cap.
I ate a million Hiawatha crumbs
And curled up for my Winter's nap.

Years later, when I came across my mother's scrapbook, I sent a copy of the poem to my niece, by then Mrs. David Scanlon of Orleans, Massachusetts. It brought back memories to her of the days when the club met in members' homes, starting when they did Red Cross work each week, rolling bandages and such. The schoolhouse's kitchen was not convenient for heating flat irons to sterilize the old sheets they tore up and rolled into bandages.

She recalls the incident when she was five or six and the ladies sent their children to play in the old apple orchard behind the house.

"We found a group of beautiful little black and white kitties playing. Riker Robinson, a few years older, Helen Paetzold, my best friend, and I each picked up one in each hand, by their tails, and went to the meeting."

"Well, such a furor. Leona Paetzold fainted, they all shrieked and we were in disgrace. Through the years, if I happened to see Riker when I visited Owego he'd begin to laugh and tell the story again."

After we moved to Binghamton, Verna wrote me often. She sent her own poem, written after the house was well-aired.

> Kurrit, kurrit, kurrale,
> The cat sat on a rail,
> Along came a pretty skunk
> With a bushy tail.
> The cat said mee–you,
> The skunk said it too
> But the funny way he said it
> Made the cat say whee–you.

In the early twenties, the old school house became a social club for Hiawatha families with children, with potluck suppers, square dances where little girls danced with big brothers, uncles and dads, and sumptuous holiday parties taking place under its roof.

CHAPTER 14

More Than One Cradle

We had two cradles on the Island — some of the time. My infant bed was often on loan to the youngest child among our neighbors and extended family. It wasn't made or bought for me, either. I was one in a long series of rock–a–bye–babies. It became known as Mertie and Lynn's, since we had storage space and everybody knew where to go to get it or to return it.

The rockers were low and slightly S–curved at the ends, so it was not easily upturned. A grandma, mother, or sibling could be shelling peas, mending clothes, knitting socks, and still keep the cradle in motion by toe–tapping.

This cradle served Scott and Verna's Mary Janeth, and later, Scott, Jr. after my brother, Elmo, outgrew it. When, at 23, I expected my first child, the same cradle got a fresh coat of bright blue paint. Dad Snedaker remarked that after so many years, perhaps it was the paint that held it together. Who knows? Some antique lover may have finally removed the rockers and set her potted plants in it.

The other island cradle was seldom borrowed. In fact, it didn't get used. Quite probably, it was hanging on its peg in the horse barn when we moved there, left over from the heyday of hotel provendering. Logic didn't stop me from fantasizing that Grandpa Cornelius and his sons had used it in the home fields of Ingraham Hill, near Binghamton, especially after Dad explained to me just how it was done.

This cradle was an arrangement of parallel wooden rods to attach to a scythe blade so the heads of rye, wheat, oats, buckwheat, or whatever all fell in the same direction. It was not likely I'd ever see a crew of five or six threshers at work, so I listened, closed my eyes, and watched. The men began as soon as the dew had dried. Starting at the left side, the leader grasped the snath with both hands and struck in with a wide swing from the right, then dumped the cut grain to the left with a cock of his elbow.

Two steps and repeat, two steps and repeat, leaving a neat windrow.

The second man started after the leader's sixth pass and the others in succession. Their rhythmic line stretched in a diagonal across the field. Should the end mower be a fast one, the whole line sped up to save their heels! Needless to say, no left–handed scythers were in the line. Once a man reached the far border of the field, he shouldered

his scythe and walked diagonally across the cut windrows to take his place as the last man in line.

The welcome sight of a youngster coming from the farmhouse with a pail of switchel meant a quick time–out for a sweltering yeoman while he quenched his thirst with molasses–sweetened vinegar water from a tin dipper. Some housewives added the snap of a bit of ginger.

For untold generations, grasses were cut with a sickle in back-breaking labor. The crescent–shaped blade grew more slender with each honing of the stone. A short handle was attached to the end of the metal. It made no difference how the grasses fell, for grains and husks were separated by treading feet of humans and oxen at the threshing floor, as in the biblical story of Ruth and Boaz. Even today, in many developing countries, a leather flail is employed. Dad had a small sickle for cutting a path through shore grass or in the woods.

Only when some forgotten Edison decided to lengthen the blade and attach a long curved handle at a near right angle, could man walk upright in this necessary work. When Cyrus Hall McCormack developed a successful horse–drawn harvesting machine the era of vast prairie fields of waving grain became a reality.

Why did we have a scythe? Why discard something useful in mowing marsh grass? Besides, it was borrowed every year for some would–be Father Time to greet the infant New Year, but the cradle, on its peg, just got dustier.

Stereograph photo, for use in a "3-dimensional" Stereograph viewer

CHAPTER 15

My Brother, Carl

My brother, eight years my senior with no siblings between, made numerous playthings for me. Nowadays, they'd be called folk toys. He never actually gave me any because of definite ideas about keeping a pesky kid sister in line.

He notched one surface of a six–inch long, three–quarter–inch walnut stick, attached a handmade propeller blade with a brad through a bead, removed the lead pencil I was using from my hand and permitted me to watch him rub it back and forth length-wise over the notches. The propeller came to life and was soon whirling like mad.

"This stick obeys my command," he declared solemnly. "Reverse direction!" Before my amazed eyes, the blade slowed for a moment's stop then spun away as directed. Carl never varied the back–and–forth motion, but what a grin!

"Do it again," I begged. He did.

"Could I do that?" I asked.

"Probably not, but you can try."

"How do I make it go?"

"You watched me, didn't you? That's the right way to learn. Keep your eyes open and your mouth shut." Hands on hips, he gloated as I failed that first attempt, then snatched the toy and pocketed it.

"Please, please, pretty please. Show me how, please," I entreat-ed. He stalked off.

"Have to do my chores. Can't waste any more time on you."

After several days of watching and "keeping my mouth shut," I noticed that part of the time his thumb rubbed along one side of the stick. Then, with ever so slight a sideways motion, his bent index finger rubbed the other side. From then on, whenever he grumpily gave me access to what I've since heard called a whooey stick, I, too, could order, "CHANGE DIRECTION!"

Stories of witches and goblins and ghosts who bumped through the night meant Hallowe'en was near. Carl came to my bedroom door — we never went into the other's room without an invitation.

"I've got something special under my bed, " he whispered, conspiratorially. I scooted down to peek and pulled back in alarm. "Carl Snedaker, does Mamma know you've got green fire under your bed? You'll burn the house down! I'm going to tell on you!"

Carl cavorted about in glee, shaking with laughter like Peter Rabbit in the storybook whenever he outwitted Reddy Fox. "It's just foxfire! 'Twon't burn. 'Ain't hot but it glows in the dark. Looks like a haunt out there among the trees." That was my introduction to phosphorescent light caused by fungal growths on rotting stumps.

I felt like kicking him in the shins for scaring me so, but even more, I wanted to get out of there. He was mean, mean, mean. I slammed my door behind me, threw myself on the bed to pound the pillow in frustration and sob. Mother called for supper. I washed my face in cold water, smoothed back my hair, went downstairs, and snitched a piece of spice cake from Carl's plate to get even. He never said a word.

Carl didn't rob bird nests to build an egg collection and showed no enthusiasm for hunting. Instead of aiming at the feathered denizens, he'd bring down jumping grasshoppers with his BB gun. Once in a while at Mother's insistence when she was especially busy, I went along on some of his wanderings. I was allotted one BB and could have another shot when I found it again. By aiming low, I kept the search area to a minimum.

No use crying for another BB. He had no heart, just a stone. "If you can't find yours, you can either be quiet and watch me shoot or go back and sit on the porch." He'd wet his finger and hold it high to determine direction and velocity of the wind across a weedy flat space at the top of the hill, near our water reservoir. He was very good at hitting an empty tin can and letting me put it back on top of a fence post.

Carl and Dad fished from a boat at the upper end of the island and we'd be eating the catch within the hour... Carl cleaned them, Mother rolled them in seasoned cornmeal and fried them. I had first dibs on the sunnies — their white flesh so sweet to my taste, the crisp fins and tails a delight to my teeth. Those meals would be hard to produce today since they were served with tiny new potatoes and vegetables fresh from our garden and fruit from the orchard.

CHAPTER 16

Models of Ingenuity

Carl had the gift of three–dimensional imaging. He'd look at the front of an object and apparently know at once what the sides and back, the top and bottom, and even the insides were like. Part of that talent came from Dad, but Carl expanded it to uncanny expertise.

When we heard that a farmer beyond Owego was letting a barn stormer use one of his fields, we all piled into the car for a rubber-neck excursion. We pulled off the road under a fringe of trees and joined earlier arrivals to gaze expectantly into the almost cloudless sky. Sure enough, we were soon rewarded with our first ever sight of that marvelous, if impractical, contraption, a flying machine. Aeroplane was the fancied–up name. It circled the field a few times, then seemed about to roll over to one side. I learned that was called banking. It was still going at what seemed to me a pretty fast clip when it landed, raising dust in the dry ground as it slowed to a stop.

The pilot stepped out, a dashing figure in leather helmet and gog-gles and walked, laughing, to meet the surging crowd. "Who'll be the first to take a ride with me? We'll fly up high and you can see all over the countryside!"

Finally, a few of the more daring cajoled timid wives or sweet-hearts to "come along." I held my breath as the first couple climbed in. My heart beat wildly and my neck got a kink, following their giddy path in the sky. They were aloft certainly no more than five minutes and returned to earth exuding the wonder of it all.

"Lynn, we could see your cows in the back meadow on the island," the chap called. "You all looked so little from up there," his fair companion giggled nervously. Their friends gathered close, seeking courage to do it themselves.

None of us Snedakers took "the chance to be scared to death" but once we got home, Carl grabbed pencil and paper and started planning how to build an operating toy model.

Dad gave him the run of the wood shop and Mother cooperated by sacrificing our large milky–green umbrella to provide silk fabric for the biplane. Carl whittled and measured, aiming for the least possible weight yet always aware of the need for strength. How he would have loved balsa wood!

I recall the wing span as about 30 inches and a total length almost as great. The fuselage, (now, there was a word for my tongue's delight), was hollow except for powerful rubber bands stretched from the tail to a hook on the propeller. Carl made several propellers to experiment with torque and to provide replacements and he rigged up moveable flaps which he could set to control lift and flight.

He glued the wooden frame, using the smelly fish glue that Dad always kept in a pot, ready to heat to liquidity. He measured accurately and traced the pattern of the coverings on the umbrella panels, then painstakingly checked and rechecked before cutting and sewing. Mother showed him how, but Carl wielded his own needle. If memory serves me right, he tried both wooden wheels and skids. Only when the earth was well–covered with newly–fallen soft snow was the place in the mood to accept a graceful landing.

We all bundled up. I was to stay out of the way, on the side porch, which proved to be a fine location. Mother and Carl went into the yard. Carl raised his wet finger to read the wind, decided on the course of flight — toward the distant woods which surrounded Hiawatha House — and Mother held the plane while Carl turned the propeller. 'round and 'round to twist the rubber bands. Mother raised the plane above her head, while Carl kept a tight hold on the propeller. "A little higher at the front, Mother. Now, more to your right. There. Ready?"

"Ready!"

Carl shouted, "push her off!" at the same moment releasing his hold on the propeller.

She flew! Not far, but she flew, maybe 30 or 40 feet, losing altitude all the time. She landed on her nose and Carl immediately had use for one of his spare propellers. We were all so proud of him!

In a few days, another launching took place. That time, he had to replace several struts. One disastrous day, both wings on one side were splintered. The plane was out of operation for several weeks. Eventually, it ended up suspended from Carl's bedroom ceiling wherever we lived, until he married Ellen.

☆ ☆ ☆

His model submarine, inspired by the dire news of ships in the Atlantic being lost to undersea warfare, was equally ingenious, but less fun. One might follow a wake, but we would never be able to watch its path like we would something airborne. Only when the river was warm and calm enough to be almost rippleless and certainly not in flood, was it possible to launch the submarine.

Sometimes I toted the sub while Carl brought the oars. He'd put the blades inside the boat, drop the pins into the oar locks, kneel on the thwart, "power up" the sub's rubber bands, and point. "She'll come up just this side of the sand bar."

He'd push it under and off, then row as fast as he could to retrieve her. The current was always strong along the bar and he didn't want his creation carried downstream. He didn't want her to get water–logged, either.

If she didn't show, he'd drop anchor and jump into the river, hence his swim suit attire. Could be that the rubber bands had broken under stress. Something floating or sunken beneath the surface might have deflected her path. The rotor blade could be snagged in eelgrass. One day. his search was unsuccessful. He didn't build a replacement.

☆ ☆ ☆

Carl had been a reliable farm hand from an early age. He

especially enjoyed dealing with problems and, at times, worked out the solution before Dad knew something was amiss. When the rest of the family went to town or on a day trip, he'd usually opt to stay home "and see to the chores and things."

He never complained about anything being too difficult or unfair. On one beautifull summer day, we could hear kids camped on the mainland shore laughing and calling boisterously. Carl hoisted a coil of wire onto his shoulder and went to mend a weak spot in the far corner of the pasture fence. Dad was in the field.

Mother and I were busy in the kitchen when the hired man ran pell–mell towards the house, shouting frantically that Carl was hurt bad. Carl had supposed that the big, irascible breeder bull was in the other pasture. He'd been out of sight, over the river bank. The boys in their flotilla of canoes, city kids who didn't know better, harried the bull, flapping their stripped–off shirts and screaming with glee when he started pawing the earth. He couldn't reach the campers, so he started running back and forth, then right over the top of the bank.

And there was Carl. He'd just climbed over the fence and was still encumbered by the weighty wire. The bull tossed him, then sank his horn into the fallen victim's shoulder.

The hero of the hour was our quick–witted hired man. He heard the bellowing, grabbed a fresh fence post, and rushed to help. Keeping the sturdy post between him and them, he belabored the bull's back side until the enraged creature turned his fury on him. Carl managed somehow to slip out of the coil and start crawling under the fence. He was bleeding badly. The good samaritan grabbed his arms and pulled him several rods away to temporary safety.

An alarm blast on Mother's tin fish horn brought Dad in a hurry. He grabbed his gun and shot the rampaging behemoth before he could break out to wreak more havoc.

The two men dared not lift and carry Carl lest they add to his considerable injuries. They supported him, upright, as he stumbled to the back porch where he collapsed.

That was the first time I ever saw my brother cry.

He was whimpering with pain. Mother scooped the chunk of ice from the top of the icebox and into the sink. "Eupha, wash that off good. We'll need it." She ran to get clean towels and blankets.

Mother got Central on the phone. "This is Mertie Snedaker. We are on the way to Owego with Carl. He's been gored."

"I'll take care of everything, Mertie. You get going!"

Dad had the car cranked up, with Carl in it. Mother cradled his head in her lap and pressed the wrapped cake of ice, hard against the bloodiest part of his shoulder. There's no way to tourniquet a shoulder. She piled on blankets to keep him warm and lessen the shock.

The hired man helped pull the ferry across, then returned in the spare boat to stay with me. The poor fellow was completely spent. He sank down on the couch and mercifully slept.

I cried myself dry. My brother was dying or already dead.

It was evening before I found I'd been wrong. Carl came back home with Mom and Dad — there was no hospital in or around Owego then. I wouldn't have known Carl, bandaged like an Egyptian mummy with every place that showed black and blue , and so swollen that his eyes were hidden.

Eventually, his pitifully splintered shoulder blade healed under Mother's skillful care, but nothing could truly restore it. His shoulder and arm stayed in a permanent slough and his suits never fit very well for the rest of his life.

Still, he never complained.

NOTE: At that time, rural areas didn't even have aspirin to relieve the pain. That came out of the first World War. We didn't have x-rays either. What we did have was doctors who cared, parents who loved, and neighbors who were concerned. And we had faith.

The Rainbow

Boats sail on the rivers,
    And ships sail on the seas;
But clouds that sail across the sky
    Are prettier far than these.

There are bridges on the rivers,
    As pretty as you please;
But the bow that bridges heaven,
    And overtops the trees,
And builds a road from earth to sky,
    Is prettier far than these.

CHRISTINA ROSSETTI

CHAPTER 17

Rainbow of Crayons

Did ever a child open a brand new box of Crayola ™ crayons and not try out each one fast? My many–banded rainbow used all but the white one. With black, I printed the name.

Carl came by. I bent to shield my picture. He'd never say it was pretty or nice.

"That's no Roy G. Biv."

"Course not. It's not a man, it's a rainbow!"

"If you're going to draw a rainbow right, you'd better learn how to make Roy G. Biv. Say it!"

"Don't want to!"

"Okay. Spell it."

"R–O–Y–G–B–I–V." Pride commanded I show off my phonics.

"Now, listen and learn, Small Fry. R is Red — that's the color of the longest band, the one on top. Next one is O for Orange. Then Y . . ."

I interrupted. "Y is Yellow. It's the only color that starts with Y."

"You're so smart, what's G?"

"Can't be gray. I don't have a gray crayon. Oh, it's Green . . . but there's lots of B colors — black, brown, blue . . ."

"Which is in the rainbow?"

"Hasta be Blue." I puckered my brow. "There isn't any I color."

"It's a new word for you. Indigo." He picked up the purplish–blue crayon. "And it's spelled I–N–D–I–G–O."

"V must be Violet."

"Right – O, Kid – O. What's the name of the rainbow?"

"Roy G. Biv. But some rainbows have just three or four colors, pale ones. Remember that bright one last week? That was a real Roy G. One end touched the hills near Campville, and the other over the river, around Apalachin."

"Sure. That was Wednesday afternoon, the day of the gully washer. We went outside to look as soon as the storm slacked off, and you stood staring towards the sun instead of turning your back to him." Always cutting me down to size.

Mother approved my drawing. Patting the couch seat next to her, we opened a book.

Noon has no rainbows. The sun is straight above. Morning when the sun is in the east, rainbow's in the west. Afternoons, the bow is in the east and if I could be away up high in a balloon, I just might see a whole circle instead of half of one.

"Oh, I didn't know this."

Eagerly, Mother launched into other names for rainbows: in Italy, the flashing arch; in France, the arch in the sky; in faraway Asia, the little window in the sky, or the bow of India. Some North African tribes greet the bride of the rain.

An old European belief held that when a saint dies, his soul transits from earth to heaven on that glowing bridge. It's the bridge of the Holy Spirit, the girdle of God, the arch of St. Martin, the crown of St. Bernard.

The first rainbow of all was set in the sky after the flood, as God's bright promise that never again would He destroy the earth by water.

At Hiawatha, we sometimes saw faint bows in the river fog. When we visited the falls and cascades of Montour or Watkins Glen, there were rainbows in the mist. We even had some indoors as the sun shone through the cut–glass prisms on the parlor lamp, and thousands more in my crayon box.

EMB.

A wasp met a bee that was buzzing by,

And he said, "Little cousin, can you tell me why

You are loved so much better by people than I?

"My back shines as bright and yellow as gold,

And my shape is most elegant, too, to behold;

Yet nobody likes me for that, I am told."

"Ah, cousin," the bee said, "'tis all very true;

But if I had half as much mischief to do,

Indeed they would love me much better than you.

"You have a fine shape and a delicate wing;

They own you are handsome; but then there's one thing

They cannot put up with, and that is your sting.

"My coat is quite homely and plain, as you see,

Yet nobody ever is angry with me,

Because I'm an humble and innocent bee."

From this little story let people beware,

Because like the wasp, if ill natured they are,

They will never be loved, if they're ever so fair.

SUNBEAMS, ©1889

CHAPTER 18

A Hornet's Nest For Sure

People often ask if dangerous wild things lived on the Island. YES! Thousands of them, winged and vicious if disturbed. An unusually large paper wasp nest hung low one year, on a branch above the path from our kitchen to the ice house. Dad cut a new swath for detour. Everyone who came to visit was warned. Even cats and dogs instinctively avoided the area, since these were what Dad accurately if inelegantly called white–assed hornets, the terror-ists of the entire wasp clan. They are also white-faced. The biggest were almost an inch and a half long.

That was one of several years when we hosted a family reunion.

Long tables were set outdoors on the opposite side of the house, convenient to our kitchen where the women were busy with food for the spread.

Menfolk swapped stories or wandered out towards the horse barn to pitch horseshoes. Some manned the ferry since families were still arriving.

Kids dashed about in raucous games of hide–and–go–seek. One almost collided with Verna carrying two large glass pitchers of iced lemonade, so they were banished to the lawn near the porch.

The boisterous fun continued. "Devious" reasoned that no one would look for him behind the forbidden tree and they didn't find him. The hornets did.

Hundreds of hornets streamed out of their nest for a territorial attack, buzzing furiously. Unlike bees' barbed stingers, which are usually left in the victim, hornet stingers are bigger and sharper. They wound over and over again. The chemical component of the venom is singuarly virulent. "Devious" screamed and tried to run away, but fell to the ground, unconscious.

How they rescued the child without others falling victim, I don't know. The women somehow revived him and when they had, he wished they hadn't. He couldn't even cry for his eyes were swollen shut. His ears stood out from his head like misplaced rhinoceros horns. He could only moan.

"Lynn, you ought to get rid of that nest," someone called. Dad turned to look him in the eye.

"How?"

☆ ☆ ☆

Fortunately, hornets do not live through the winter, except for fertilized new young queens. Dad waited for the third hard frost. He, with his saw, and Carl, carrying a giant burlap sack, finished the chapter.

First, Dad removed the branch beyond the nest, then sawed it off completely on the trunk side. They deposited it in the bag, dragged it to the shore, and loaded it with the heaviest stones there. Dad rowed out, well beyond the sandbars and heaved it over.

If any queens were still inside, you can be sure none of their progeny ever emerged.

CHAPTER 19

Nursemaiding Turkeys

Once Mr. Marvin heard about the rather spectacular enterprises of turkey ranching in unsettled foothill regions in the west and learned that Midwest housewives were raising small flocks for local Thanksgiving and Christmas demand, it was no—whoa but that he should present Mother with a clutch of large, freckled turkey eggs.

Mr. Marvin saw it as a side issue to her regular work and a nice bonus for her at sell–off time. "If you winter over only a half–dozen turkey hens and a gobbler, you can raise a flock of 40 to 50 turkeys. The Department of Agriculture is enthusiastic as to the possibilities."

She thanked him kindly, but in ensuing hassles wished she'd dropped and broken the whole nest full in surprise!

Finding a broody hen for a surrogate mother was easy. She confined her inside an upended wooden crate until dark, then put half the eggs under her on a bed of straw. After an uneasy night sitting on eggs uncommonly large, Biddy settled down, and that evening, Mother slipped the rest of the clutch under her.

I've read that 1916 Agriculture Yearbook, starting with accounts from California and Arizona. I quote:

> *Here the range is unlimited and the natural food of the turkey, such as grasshoppers and other insects, green vegetation, and the seeds of various weeds and grasses, is abundant.*
>
> *Advantage also is taken of the turkey's relish for acorns,and where these are plentiful but a little grain need be used for fattening in the fall.*
>
> *These large flocks of turkeys are managed much like herds*

*of sheep , being taken out to the range early in the morning
and brought home to roost at night. They are herded during
the day by men, either on foot or on horseback and by dogs
especially trained for the work.*

Poor Mother. She had the turkeys, but not the herders. The
fowls' appetites. as described, were diverted to garden greenery and
meadow clover, much preferable to rank weeds! Further, creatures
which instinctively roost high in the trees, above the reach of
predators, were almost impossible to keep penned.

*Toward the latter part of winter or early in the spring the
turkey hens begin laying, and then comes the task of finding
the nests, which are usually well–hidden in a patch of weeds
or in a bushy thicket, sometimes half a mile away. The
inexperienced turkey grower may spend hours in following a
turkey hen before her nest is discovered, but to the initiated*
(which Mother was not!), *this is a simple task.*

*By confining all the hens early some mornings and letting
them out late in the afternoon, those that are laying will
strike out on a run for their respective nests, and the secret
of their hiding places can be quickly and easily learned."*
(By one lone woman, on top of her regular work?)

*After the nests are found, the eggs are gathered daily and
kept safe from any danger of becoming chilled or from being
destroyed by a dog, skunk, opossum, rat, crow, or other
enemy. As soon as each turkey hen has finished laying her
litter of about 18 eggs and has become broody, a nest is carefully prepared and from 15 to 20 eggs are given her to incu-
bate.*

*After 28 days of sitting, the poults appear, and for the
next few weeks they must be fed and looked after frequently,
and above all they must be protected from dampness, for if
they become wet and chilled their chance of living is small
indeed.*

Mother maintained that she never had a mother turkey with
enough sense to call her poults under her wings and protect them
from a pouring rain. They were all for Number One and flew into

a leafy tree to sit out the unpleasantness while my mother scurried about, collecting miserable young ones in her apron and drying them off with towels in the kitchen in front of an open oven.

As soon as the poults were feathered,

> *"there is little danger that they will not then survive and from this time on until the turkeys are marketed in the fall, the greatest difficulty . . . is to keep the birds from ranging too far and causing trouble with the owners of neighboring farms."*

I'm sure Mr. Marvin read that and thought the wide Susquehanna would serve well.

> *"About the first of October, the fattening season is begun by gradually increasing the amount of grain, usually corn, thrown to the turkeys just before roosting time. A week or two before marketing they receive all the grain they will clean up two or three times a day. . . between Thanksgiving and Christmas turkeys are found to be more easily fattened . . . they have attained the greater part of their growth. . . the weather is cooler and there is less to tempt them to range so widely..."*

True, Mr. Marvin, but let's sell them when they aren't quite so fat. We need time to get the family, house, and farm ready for Christmas!

Do you suppose those turkeys were the reason I got to stay overnight with Scott and Verna? Mother did a good job at whatever she set her mind to and reared a large percentage of hatchlings each year. She earned every cent she made. When a 40 pound gobbler spread his iridescent fantail to strut the yard and gobble loudly, he was a sight for sore eyes and a subsequent feast for the table.

A Hiawatha Island Childhood 1911 – 1919

CHAPTER 20

The Farm Cellar

Supermarkets do not go back as far as my childhood. A farm family provided its own store of good hearty food, down cellar. A lot of sowing and hoeing and timely picking went into feeding the family well, and young and old joined in the effort. That was the normal way of life in self–sufficient rural America.

Our cellar was dim, dark, and cool, with a slightly woodsy smell from its packed dirt floor. Even in midwinter, you could sense last summer's rains. The moisture content of the air factored significantly in successful storage of fruits and root crops. As one opened the door at the top of the stairs, heady fragrances assailed the nostrils. It was a tantalizing promise of plenty, the spice of pickles curing in crocks, the richness of apples and cider, the down–to–earth aroma of potatoes dug from the brown earth and cured by autumn breezes before being sorted into bushel baskets. (Early red potatoes were eaten as they were dug.) There was the fruitiness of a weeping glass of grape or plum jelly and perhaps the slightly sour undertone of sauerkraut and the tanginess of nuts.

One went down the stairs carefully, carrying a lamp or lantern, preferably the latter, easy to hang on an S–shaped hook embedded in an overhead beam. Our cellar was typical, with a row of barrels down the middle, sturdy shelves along the facing walls, racks for bottles and crocks, and a jelly cupboard or two with side–hinged doors to discourage mice. Their sensitive noses first sought out the paraffin with which the glasses were sealed, then, if still undetected in their gourmet dining, they gorged themselves on the contents. One time, a mouse chewed a hole through the corner of a cupboard, and Mother told Dad, who promptly cut a patch from a tin can, bent it, and nailed it in place. I never forgave the forager who ate a whole jar of grape frappe made with Concords, hickory nuts, and walnuts. I'd helped pick those nut meats out of their retentive shells!

Shelves for home–canned fruits and vegetables had to be sturdy. They carried a lot of weight in those quart and half–gallon Ball or Mason jars. They didn't have to be fancy — unplaned planks worked fine. A thick newspaper covering did double duty, to guard against splinters and to simplify clean–up if a jar fermented and spilled or broke. Hanging shelves suspended from the ceiling posed a hazard for the impatient. Both sides were open, making it far too easy to push something off the far edge.

Some folks stored root crops out–of–doors by digging a cave into a side hill. They spread carrots, beets, turnips, potatoes, even cabbages and buried them in deep straw, then mounded the earth high to insulate against frost. However, we had sufficient cellar room for crates, bins, and barrels, and even a sand-filled box where Mother wintered flower bulbs and tubers, especially gladiolas and dahlias.

Dad favored a particular patented crate, made of wooden slats and hinged at the corners. The base too was hinged at one end and at the opposite end rested on a heavy strip of wood for support. Lift the base when emptied and the whole device folded to save storage space. He thought about such things and was expert in saving time, materials, and energy as well. I remember going downstairs for a bowl of apples for the evening snack. "Look for any with spots and bring them up. One bad apple can spoil a whole crateful."

Great Granddad countermanded with, "Always bring the best apples you can find. Even when they all get spots, we'll be eating the best of the batch."

Individuality evidenced its happy self in what a woman chose to put by, beyond the basics. Carry–ins, picnics, and reunions boasted chili sauce, pepper relish, spiced pears, green tomato, dill, sweet, and bread–and–butter cucumber pickles. Watermelon rind was my favorite, made with oil of cloves and oil of cinnamon, with a several–morning ritual of draining off the syrup and bringing it to a boil, then putting the pared rind squares back in for another day's absorption of spicy, vinegary sweetness.

The Island was ideal for a large field of watermelons — less depredation. "Anyone too lazy to grow his own melon is too lazy to row a boat to get it." Nothing was more refreshing on a hot day than one of those big buggers chilled in a washtub full of ice!

Canning season began with spring peas. We started shelling them when we finished asparagus. We ate all we grew of that! Smooth–skin peas went in the ground before it was bare of snow, crinkled ones in another week or ten days All were tender with moisture. "They're so good with little new potatoes. We eat all we can and can all we can't."

Out came a big oval copper boiler with a wooden rack in the bottom to keep jars from breaking during processing. Mom didn't like us to ever play with the domed copper cover, but it was a temptation. Its wooden handle in the center was just right to carry as a knight's shield..

Somewhere along the line, Mom got a new–fangled canner, a pressure cooker, despite its bad publicity. Anyone could tell her of somebody someone else knew (never first–hand knowledge!) who'd been scalded "just awful." Let the stove get a bit too hot and "whoosh." Off would go the pressure valve, not only releasing super–hot steam, but pulling liquid from the jars as well. Mother maintained that if you paid attention, you finished the job in jig time. Food was less apt to spoil as well. It may have been after we moved from the Island that she switched.

After peas came green beans, the string–me kind. We grew a few pale yellow ones, mainly for pickling whole.When beans got too big for table use, they stayed on the vine to ripen and harden into shell beans. Most were shucked and stored in paper sacks in the attic. Some, like the string beans, were canned; others were married to corn as succotash.

Corn was a winter mainstay, dozens of quarts of Golden Bantam. I was too young to help cut kernels from cobs, so I pestered Mom, "Why does the back of the blade get all gooey when you scrape the cob?"

"The milk is sticky, like sugar syrup."

"Who put sugar in it?"

Mother was exasperated. "It grew in it. Now, be quiet while I fill these jars."

She used a wide–mouth funnel, added a teaspoon of salt and a lot of boiling water, worked air pockets from the packed corn with a silver knife blade, and capped the jars, leaving head room for heat expansion.

More dozens of jars of tomatoes provided canned sunshine over the winter. Oranges were a rarity. We couldn't have grown them in our climate, anyway. Small tomatoes ended up gingered or as candied preserves, or as catsup. Making it was a long, messy job. It needed frequent stirring or it stuck.. Scorched catsup — UGH!

"Why's it called cat soup, Mother?"

"Not soup. It's catsup, and that's its name. I have no idea why." Later, ketchup became the preferred spelling.

As frost threatened, everything was gathered in a last flurry, including little green tomatoes. If they showed a blush, or even a light streak, unblemished ones were spread out, not touching each other, on newspapers on the back room table. They ripened slowly. All–greens became green tomato mincemeat or some kind of pickle.

Except for applesauce, plain or spiced, and apple butter made from the drops that didn't go into cider, fruits were canned, straight, in a simple syrup, or mixed with nuts and raisins for sweet conserves, or pulped for jam, juiced for jelly, spiced for firm pickles.

We grew red pie cherries; purple, red, green, and yellow plums; Bartlett and Seckel pears; free–stone and cling–stone peaches, and berries galore, beginning with ripe, juicy strawberries for shortcake. I loved red raspberries with cream. Picking excursions took advantage of wild largesse.

Mother carried a special egg basket when she went to Owego to shop. The Marvin kitchen was well–supplied and other friends liked to buy from her as well. Egg money was the farmwife's mad money. When hens went on a production spree and even the storekeeper cried, "Enough," Mom put down the surplus in water-glass, technically sodium silicate.

These eggs were not washed first. That would destroy the shell's natural protection. She wiped each with a dry towel and lowered them one by one into a tall crock in the cellar, then carefully poured "soluble glass" to submerge them, excluding air. An old dinner plate, weighted with a brick, covered all.

Waterglass eggs were manna when the layers slacked off and we had barely enough fresh ones for breakfast. Farmers needed fortifying meals for mucking out and other chores. Ice and snow kept the dairy herd penned inside in straw–bedded stalls. Only one thing seldom froze — the manure pile, which steamed! By early spring, its straw content was well composted.

If Mother needed two eggs for a plain cake, or a dozen for angel food, she had them at hand. She'd plunge her arm to the elbow in the cold crock, feel about and grasp each egg positively. They were slippery as all get–out and so were her hands.

Weather settled into constant cold. Hogs were as fat as they'd ever be. — It was time to haul out the giant cauldron, hang it on a tripod or from a high beam stretched between trees, and get water boiling to scald the carcass. Our pork barrel stood to one side of the cellar stairs waiting to be refilled. Many a mid–winter meal started off by fishing out a piece of salt pork to fry and serve with potatoes and pan gravy. Crackling brine left a ridge of rime on one's goose–pimpled arm.

Butchering meant ribs to roast, rashers of bacon and hams to cure in our smokehouse over hickory coals, and sausage to grind. We didn't stuff links, but kept the sausage in pans, covered with an inch of lard.

Trying out lard was part of the scene. With fine, fresh white shortening available for melt–in–your–mouth crusts, what better time for pie–making on a monumental scale?

Traditional mincemeat used up little pieces of pork and pecks of blemished apples. Perfect pumpkins were chunked with a hatchet, then peeled, steamed, and mashed. Less–than–perfect ones went to the animals. An unheated summer kitchen kept pies ready to thaw and eat on demand. We had a more protected place too, a small room with shelves, closed off from the rest of the cellar, where the window could be left slightly ajar. Come a company meal, pies were simply heated up, leaving the oven free for roast fowl or meat, baked beans, and scalloped potatoes. We children didn't snitch hard–frozen pies. We had the cookie jar.

The poetry of pumpkins and squashes is inherent in their names. You could sing them from the seed catalog: Rhode Island Sweet! Nantucket Sugar! Golden Oblong! Michigan Mammoth! Cocozelle! Big Cheese! Golden Custard! Jumbo! Yum Yum! Quaker Pie! Chinese Alphabet! Black Sugar! Bugle Gramma! Winter Luxury!

Back in the Virginia Colonies, John Smith wasn't so fortunate. Pumpkin pies weren't yet invented when he wrote, "It is like unto a Muske Millon, but lesse and worse."

Pumpkins and squashes planted about every third hill with the field corn didn't start runners until corn rows had their final hoeing. Then they helped keep the weeds down. Harvested golden globes hardened for about a fortnight. We stored them in the barn, handy to the pigs.. They got most of them, sometimes in a mash cooked of squash slices along with potatoes too small to peel, and cornmeal.

Even in those Hiawatha Island years, times were changing. Lost heat from central heating altered conditions radically. First in cities, then in villages and on farms, electricity replaced kerosene and the gasoline motor. Drains were installed and concrete poured over the old dirt floor. The furnace and washing machine moved in. Appetizing fragrances were vanquished by the smell of laundry soap, bleach, dust, coal gas, and steam.

Hail Modernity!

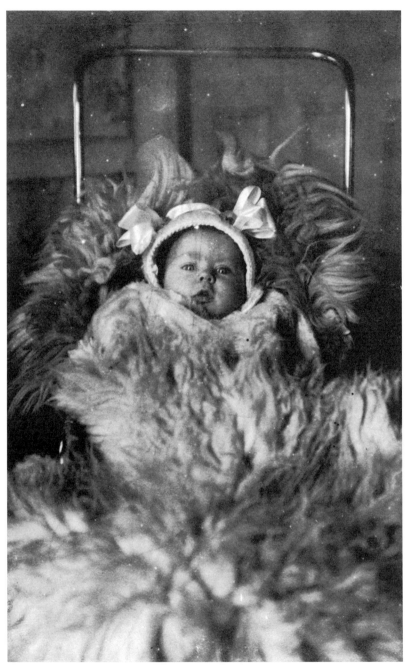

Eupha, first year on the Island

A Hiawatha Island Childhood 1911 – 1919

CHAPTER 21

In Winter

I sensed that my life was different — nicely different. No child I knew had a whole island and the freedom to wander about it. Woodchucks, squirrels, chipmunks, and rabbits watched me as I watched them. I explored, inspired by Dad's adventurous friends.

I was all ears as Father and a crony or two swapped stories during the leisure months. Field work was finished, boats stored for the season, and repairs done on leather fittings, machinery, and outbuildings. Chores involving livestock and poultry kept the day to a relaxed routine.

J. Alden Loring, Owego naturalist and taxidermist, might drive out. The river ice was thick by then, especially in the crossing which we tried to keep clear. Glare ice deepens in sub–zero weather as frost descends. Snow covering insulates. An alert driver whose horse wore calks had no difficulty in dodging low drifts and crossing safely.

Tod held me on his lap as he told of going to Africa with Teddy Roosevelt. They collected elephants, giraffes, hippos, zebras, and exotic breeds of the deer family for the Smithsonian. Mr. Loring gave me my first golden–brown plush teddy bear that I wore threadbare with loving and cuddling.

When Dad shot a large bird that was after the chickens, he discovered that it didn't have red tail hawk markings. Tod identified it as an immature American eagle, blown far from his nest in a violent storm. He mounted the specimen on a branch from a large bark–covered slab and Father installed him above his roll–top desk. To Mother's chagrin, she had another dust catcher to be feather–dusted every week. At spring and fall house cleaning, the eagle was further groomed with damp flannel cloth.

One of Dad's friends had gone north to the Yukon in the gold rush. What memories he shared! And another had trapped, traded, traveled, and lived with the Indians west of the Mississippi. An expert tracker, he got me interested in identifying tell–tale marks in the snow — the sweep of an owl's wing, the drag of a mouse's tail, pellets of feather and bone at the foot of the hollow tree where the owl hooted. *Wild Animals I have Known* and one of Carl's illustrated manuals allowed me to study further.

Grandpa Newcomb was a Union veteran, but he seldom mentioned the war. One time, though, he told of Andersonville Prison where some of his buddies were held by the Confederates, and of Elmira, the Union Army's counterpart.

☆ ☆ ☆

The first harvest of the calendar year was preceded by neither seeding, weeding, nor cultivating, yet was so massive it required its own separate storage building and so labor intensive that half the men from both sides of the river came to help and share.

Farms didn't have electricity yet. Ice harvesting was important both for the dairyman whose market milk had to be cooled and the frugal housewife who abhorred the loss of good food by spoilage through lack of refrigeration.

A Hiawatha Island Childhood   1911 – 1919

Temperatures to twenty degrees below zero were not uncommon. A good spell of such weather assured an ice depth of twelve inches or more and alerted everyone to get ready. Horses must have sharp calks on their shoes; workers needed spiked boots or crampons, which were strapped ice creepers clamped onto the thick leather soles of their heavy work shoes. Ample piles of dry wood were stacked where the shoreline curved, to fuel bonfires. A man could take off his sodden mittens and stand close, to warm his fingers and toes before they turned blue.

The whole cutting area had to be scraped clear of debris and drifts in advance and one kept his fingers crossed against the winds swirling loose snow back again. It was too cold for new snow to fall.

The ice plow was weighted with heavy stones for deep grooves and pulled by our sturdy team. Dad drove, scoring parallel lines across the whole work area. Then he changed direction to a right angle to make yard–square blocks. Getting the first ones out was difficult. The men attacked with special ice saws in order to grab a block with multi–jointed tongs. Lines fastened to the team's traces helped. They worked in a straight row from shore to make a channel for the rest of the blocks, broken off with crowbars, to be floated to the waiting sledge. One memorable year, the ice was so deep that each block had to be cross–sawed before it could be hauled.

Commercial ice houses usually stood near the water but the Island's stood against the steep hill behind Hiawatha House, shaded by trees and convenient to the hotel kitchen and pantry. It was capacious to hold enough to satisfy the demands of the resort's chef, which were numerous at the height of the season. We had a longer but well–worn path to our place.

Carl usually helped with piling the blocks onto a sledge at water's edge, towing it to the building, and carefully stacking the blocks, packing fresh sawdust around each, and tamping it into place. A surprisingly small amount of ice was lost to melting or evaporation.

The building was insulated on all sides. It had standard double walls and double doors separated by a vestibule. The outer door was closed before the inner one was opened to conserve the chilled air. It had a concrete floor with an iron grill over a drain at the lowest point. The drainpipe's S–curve formed a water barrier against the entrance of snakes (we had only a few), chipmunks, and other small animals and the outside air.

The men took home all the ice they wanted or could transport. Some lacked enough storage space to last beyond the Fourth of July, but we were more fortunate and never ran out. That may be one reason the family reunions were held on the Island several times.

The harvest was always exciting. One year we had extra, un-wanted drama. A horse broke through the ice and almost pulled its driver along with it. Safety precautions paid off, for all horses had choke lines around their necks. The driver immediately pulled the line, which kept air inside the creature's belly and she popped back up to the surface. Extra planks and super–human brawn rescued her. She lay on her side while horse blankets were used like rough towels to restore heat and circulation. A great cheer went up when she struggled to her feet. In a few days she was eating and working normally again.

I wonder. Did she have nightmares?

☆ ☆ ☆

Carl built his iceboat for action, not beauty. Rudimentary in the extreme, it was little more than skate blades attached to a beam, a sturdy mast braced onto a crosspiece, some kind of tiller, a mere excuse for a seat, and lots of canvas. He'd face into a gale that, in summer, would keep sailboats at anchor, tack several times cross-ways of the river and then, with the wind at his back, practically fly. What if his arms, legs, and ears went numb from the cold, what if his face glowed ruddy and chapped — he was having fun and I insisted on having my share.

Finally, he relented. "Stand behind me. Put your arms around my waist and hold on tight. I mean tight!" We were off!

I will attest that given a sail, a conveyance takes on a life of its own. That iceboat could rear up like a hound treeing a raccoon, bounce like a kangaroo, buck like a Brahma bull,, skitter sideways like a scared cat confronting a bulldog, and speed like a challenged thoroughbred in the last lap of a hard–run race.

Off I went and there I was, flat on my back, gasping to draw enough air into my lungs to scream after Carl. He was a quarter–mile upstream already and gaining fast. With nobody to hear me, I saved my breath. Tears would immediately freeze on my eyelids and cheeks, so I choked back the impulse and trudged homeward.

My brother didn't get to Campville that day. He finally missed me, and started tacking downstream, looking everywhere. He beached the boat and rushed to tell Mother he'd lost me.

I was sitting at the table, thawing out, with my hands in a wash basin of tepid water and my feet in a small tub set on a footstool to bring it within reach. I smiled impishly and reached for another just–from–the–oven molasses cookie. The table was almost covered with them spread on clean linen to cool. Mother stood at the range, making hot cocoa Carl devoured his growing boy's share of both, practicing what Mother always preached, "What's done is done, and cannot be undone. Least said, soonest mended." Makes for a peaceful household. Carl rightly suspected I'd learned my lesson. I didn't want to ride on his old iceboat ever again.

CHAPTER 22

Keeping Warm

We never tried to keep as warm in winter as we were in the summer. We didn't want to. In July and August, horses sweat, men perspire, and ladies glow. Clothes stick to your back. You bathe a lot and look forward to the cool of evening. Dish towels and bath towels go sour or mildew without warning. Clothes that are washed — and there are a lot of them in summer — must be ironed — another hot job. Fall is fine.

Well before the first snowflake, Dad banked the house to above floor level with dried leaves or straw though nothing could prevent all floor drafts. We wore felt shoes or padded house slippers indoors, and kept our feet high with footstools or ottomans when relaxing. Strategically within reach were shawls, sweaters, and lap robes — small woolen blankets, lined fur pieces, or colorful knit afghans. Balding husbands and grandfathers donned indoor head-gear and nightcaps. Remember? "Mamma in her kerchief and I in my cap had just settled down for a long winter's nap." A woman's crowning glory, her long hair coiled atop her head, shielded her from the cold. Incidentally, outdoorsmen favored whiskers, beards and mustaches for the same reason. To sensitize the face by scrap-ing it with a straight razor seemed folly.

When winter settled into its frigid period, one didn't remove underwear at bedtime, just stripped down to it, donned warm nightclothes, dived between flannel sheets, and piled on the quilts.

We didn't sweat much then. Bedding and underthings could go several weeks without washing. We probably developed body odors, but one's nose adjusted to that and wasn't offended by other people's either. The flannel sheets were often blue or pink plaids, or woven in multicolor strips and all in one long piece.

When folded, ends together, the fold tucked in at the bottom of the mattress. This made for a snug bed but an unwieldy armful for scrubbing on a washboard and wringing by hand. In a washing machine of that era, sheets tangled, and resisted going through the hand–cranked rubber wringer rollers.

Everything was natural fiber — cotton and wool the most widely used, silk favored more by city folk, linen only for those willing to stand for hours at the ironing board. Linen wrinkled if you looked at it sideways, Grandma Newcomb said.

Dad told of his mother's raising the flax, spinning the yarn, weaving the fabric, and making him an all–linen suit for a special occasion. "There I was, all spazzled out, walking to the gathering, when a storm cloud saw me. The first five rain drops and that suit was wet all over." We wore mostly cotton and/or wool.

We had innumerable ways to stay comfortable: winter under-wear, for example. Folks were divided in their loyalties. Some wanted one–piece union suits "because they don't leave a bare strip around the waist." Others favored separate pants and shirts, "They are easier to get into, easier to wash and dry, and lots easier for going to the bathroom." One–piecers had pull–apart flaps or barn–door drop seats. I found it hard to fasten the button in the middle of my back and time-consuming to work the side buttons.

I usually undressed in the kitchen and left clothes on a chair. Next morning, I put on my slippers and beacon cloth robe, grabbed the no-longer-hot water bottle, and hurred downstairs. Mom had my clothes warming in the oven. That really helped unless I encountered bone buttons, always hot to the touch when the fabric was just comfortable.

Petticoats and dresses were little problem once I learned to tell front from back, but oh, those long brown cotton stockings! To pull them up over underwear while keeping it around my ankles required more defenses than I could muster. One had to side–fold the ankle cuff and hold it in place. I often needed assistance to avoid being Miss Lumpy of 1916.

We wore high–laced shoes and woe to she who didn't make cer-tain that the tongue was pulled up and smoothed. How proud I was when I mastered tying a bow knot.. "Tuck the lacing ends through the loops. If they accidentally get untied, you're less apt to trip."

Men and boys wore rubber boots. I had felt gaiters, fastened with a button hook, and low rubbers. Many a time, snow packed into the button holes and turned to ice, and there was I, trying to get them off with fingers blue from the cold. Unless they were shaken clean and left to dry, they'd be cold and clammy next time. When galoshes came along with adjustable metal ladder snap fasteners, I appreciated them and never let them flap.

Sleighs and cars were open, but we had a wonderful discovery — the soapstone. We bought it, already dressed to size, an inch and a quarter thick, eight inches wide, ten inches long, with pits bored on either side near one end to hold a heavy wire bail. Soapstone is a mined talc, naturally gray and easily cut until air–hardened. Then it takes on a gentle polish. Its great virtue is holding heat over a long period. Unlike a hot water bottle which freezes if left on the floor of a vehicle, it's safe and heavy enough to stay in place. Pushed to the back of the range or placed in the oven, it heated without fear of scorching. Mother wrapped it in several layers of newspaper and we rode to town, our feet and legs toasty–warm beneath the travel robes. Further, when we took prepared oven dishes to the club or when visiting, the same soapstone in the bottom of the basket kept the food bubbly hot. I have seen a soapstone that was dropped and shattered into oblivion, but I still have ours and use it on occasion.

Kitchen salt came in two–pound, stitched cloth bags. An unopened bag, heated in the oven, held heat well too. So did baked potatoes, fresh from the oven. A kid could slip two into his pockets to keep his hands warm while sledding.

I felt very loved and cared for when Mother fixed a water bottle for me at bedtime. She'd pour from the tea kettle, leaving good headroom, then press out all the air before screwing in the stopper. On the way to my bed, she'd gather a fresh Turkish towel from the bathroom closet and wrap the bottle so it wouldn't touch my flesh, then slip it between clammy sheets, saying, "If your feet are warm, soon you'll be warm all over." I even glowed inside.

Carl used one of Mother's flatirons. She had three, and a slip–on–and–off handle. It was too heavy and awkward in shape for me to carry back down each morning.

We had a movable kerosene heater with a top bail, not much different from the upright tubular ones still being sold. We didn't like to use it much because of the fumes, but it came in very handy on bath nights.

Robert Louis Stevenson's poems were read both at home and at school.

> How do you like to go up in a swing
> Up in the air so blue?
> Oh, I do think it the pleasantest thing
> Ever a child can do.

I liked to swing. I like the verse, but I disagree with R.L.S. on that one. Surely, "the pleasantest thing" is to come from the cold, thoroughly chilled, into the blessed warmth of home.

With mittened hands and caps
        drawn low ,
    To guard our necks and ears
        from snow ,
We cut the solid whiteness through.
And where the drift was deepest,
        made
A tunnel walled and overlaid
With dazzling crystal.
                    John Greenleaf Whittier

CHAPTER 23

Dad's Fifth Automobile

My parents were, in every sense, marriage partners. Dad might lay down the law to us kids, but I never knew him to order Mother about or "absolutely forbid" her. Part of his respect showed in that she was always "Mertie" to him and "your mother" to Harry, Verna, Carl, and me. They always reached agreement on money matters, schedules, child–rearing, and vacations.

When it came to cars though, Dad went solo. He didn't know when he left to collect rents in Binghamton, that he was destined to see a vehicle that he positively had to have! He made the swap and paid the "to boot" on the spot and drove the new vehicle home. That's when I saw Mother deal with frustration.

It was just, "Lynn, wouldn't the old car have been all right for another year?"

"Tell you what, Mertie. Let's pack a picnic and go over to Pottersville, Pennsylvania this Saturday." Mother was born in Pottersville and still had aunts, uncles, and cousins living there. "You'll see how much better this car takes the hill at Devil's Elbow and it's roomier for the family."

Mother baked a loaf cake because it would travel best, boiled potatoes for salad and a dozen eggs which I helped devil, made two big thermoses of lemonade with lots of ice, and know what? We did have much more leg room and the car went right over the top of the hill in second gear!

The local correspondent sent a notice to The *Owego Gazette*: "Lynn Snedaker, of Hiawatha Island, has purchased his fifth automobile." That rigged Dad at first, but he laughed it off — "Why didn't she say, made his fifth swap?"

Another foible that bothered Mother was having Dad pull out a roll of bills big enough to choke a horse to pay for something, in the presence of strangers. A little caution was always sensible, even though crime was no big problem. Furthermore, money should be given the chance to earn interest. She always managed to have a reserve in a savings account that she was reluctant to draw on. But Dad, eleven years older than Mother, remembered that banks had failed during the last panic.

We'd go riding just to get a noseful of fresh air and an eyeful of people. Often, we'd make a stop to visit a house–bound relative or lodge brother or sister. I've known clergy who couldn't stand being in a sickroom, but Dad, with his serene sense of optimism, was a tonic to the discouraged. I'd be right beside him until the time came for paying my respects and hoping ". . . you'll be feeling better soon." Then I made myself scarce. Children were supposed to be seen and not heard.

But oh, the tales I heard! Dad soon had the invalid shedding years, reminiscing on earlier days and ways. My eager ears had me adventuring too, tracking a bear, encountering a quilled porcupine!

Visiting Uncle Jim — that's James Malone Snedaker — was exciting,. He and Aunt Nell lived in one of those small houses perched precariously on stilts, between the Johnson City–Endicott highway and a bend in the river. January and spring floods gradually eroded the bank and claimed the cottages, one by one. Theirs stood until they no longer had need of it.

A couple of times, we found George F. Johnson seated at Jim's bedside. He came every week. The two became buddies when they were young and worked at the same factory bench in what was then Lestershire. George F. had gone on to become our local industrial giant and have the name of the town changed to Johnson City after him, while Uncle Jim was afflicted with Bright's disease, a terminal kidney ailment. Such are the vagaries of fate.

Of all the Snedaker boys, Jim and Dad were most alike: ever cheerful, ever maintaining mind superiority over bodily weakness. Few people knew that Dad had lost not only the sight , but even the eyeball of one eye in a roofing accident.

Until the day of his death, Uncle Jim had a uniform response to, "How're you doing today?" He was always, "Just fine, thank you." even when Aunt Nell took us aside to tell us that the doctor had just drawn off fluid threatening his heart again that week. General belief held that a patient couldn't survive a fourth "tapping." To my best recollection, he did not succumb until after his 27th!

Aunt Nell was a widow when they married.. Before her first marriage, she had been a "bound girl," like a slave to a prosperous family who exacted endless housework of her instead of allowing her to go to school. Her native intelligence and love of reading compensated well. "When I was thirteen, they let me get baptized and join the Episcopal Church. My birth name was Eleanor, but Nellie was on everybody's lips because of a popular song. When I was asked my name at the sprinkling, I answered, 'Nellie.' " "Sometimes," she smiled wistfully, "I 've thought Eleanor better for a grown woman.

Her marriage to a merchant years older than she, was arranged. They lived on Binghamton's Canal Street when the barges were still active and drunken canallers made the nights hideous with their revelry. In my time, the canal had been filled in, paved, and renamed State Street. One sidewalk was as much as a yard above street level. Pedestrians crossed only at the corner.

She was left a strange inheritance, for her husband owned a pineapple plantation on the Isle of Pines, off the south coast of Cuba. Years later, Castro converted it into a seagirt prison camp. While still in mourning, Aunt Nell, who had never been allowed to handle money, booked passage and went by herself to arrange new management with a man residing there. She stayed through the winter. During that time, she adopted three fledgeling green parrots, blown from their nest during a gale, and planned to bring them home with her.

"We had rough seas all the way. Oh, was I seasick. I couldn't

---

even leave my cabin, but my baby birds needed food. The cabin boy brought me bread and milk,. I had to chew it well before force–feeding them. Two died, but this one," she nodded at Jock on his pedestal perch, "has been my good friend. I taught him his first words. He's a smart one and soon picked up a vocabulary by listening. We have to watch what we say," she whispered.

I knew that to be true. No sooner was I through the front door than Jock squawked, "Hello, Eupha." He kept up the racket until I went over and spoke to him.

During the daytime, he flew around the house freely. He scorned open doors and spent much of his time on the perch. At sundown, he pecked at the door of his big cage to open it and expected Aunt Nell to cover him for the night.

On a narrow marble shelf beneath their living room pier mirror was Aunt Nell's Cuban conch shell, a big one with the pastel colors of the rainbow in its lustrous nacre lining and the voice of the surf deep down inside. I held it close to my ear. "It's just your own heartbeat's echo," my factual brother informed me, but I wouldn't be belittled by that!

☆ ☆ ☆

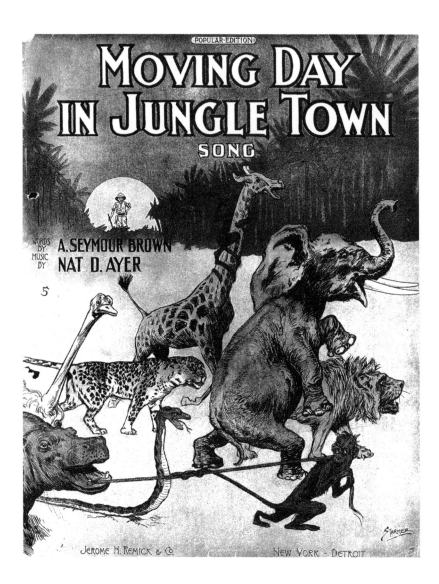

A Hiawatha Island Childhood 1911 – 1919

CHAPTER 24

To See The Elephant

Visions of places and people in their comings and goings inhabited my mind after perusing 3–D stereograph pictures, or tintypes in velvet–cased photograph albums as we visited friends and relatives.

In another home, the fabulous World's Fair of the previous decade came alive through their postcard collection. They had been there, just like the song — *Meet me in St. Louie, Louie. Meet me at the fair.* In print, of course, it was St. Louis.

"Yes," Etta had never lost the magic, "we went to see the elephant. My man came in just as I started to peel a bushel of peaches for canning. He was so excited. 'Pack our bags, Etta. I got the railroad tickets. Train leaves in four hours!'"

"Well, I pulled that bushel out to the lean–to, took off my apron, and we went. It was then or never. We missed canned sass that winter. Peaches were all rotten when we got back."

"It was worth it," her husband chimed in.

"Did you ride the Phoebe Snow?" I breathed in awe.

"Yes! Far as Buffalo and my 'gown stayed white from morn till night, upon the Road of Anthracite,' as the Lackawanna ditty promised."

"And did you see the elephant?"

"Certainly did. He was in the longest street parade I ever saw. Did you know they had over a hundred different makes of motor cars in that parade? Duryeas, Oldsmobiles, Peerlesses, Packards, Pierce Arrows, and more I'd never heard of."

Her husband's voice broke in, "Tell her about the woman who fainted."

"They brought a whole Igorot village from the Philippines and native people lived there. We gawked at them from outside the enclosure, but they didn't pay any attention to us. I sorta envied the women," she giggled. "It was hot and I was all sweated up, but they didn't wear much. They had a bunch of grown dogs and puppies running around. A man grabbed one and butchered it right there. The woman standing next to me fainted and I felt sick to my stomach."

I shuddered.

"I told her hog butchering never bothered her and the dogs were their pigs," her husband interposed.

A woman going through the Eastern Star chairs with Mother lived beyond the depot on North Street in Owego. Her son was a prison guard at Ossining on the lower Hudson, which impressed me. "I can't help fretting about the danger, him being locked in with all those murderers and other desperate criminals." She thought capital punishment a worthy idea.

"He gets home about every six weeks. He worried about me running out of wood until he had this Russian stove built." I'd been admiring the beautiful scenic tiles on a great, mostly square contrivance near an inner wall of the living room. A ledge on one side held a steaming teakettle and had room for more pots and pans. She could make tea anytime she wanted to! The humidity was refreshing — her place wasn't stuffy like some.

She explained that the inside of the masonry structure had baffles to channel fumes and smoke back and forth, back and forth, back and forth, so when they reached the chimney, their heat had been absorbed by the stove's wall. It required only a fraction of the amount of fuel needed for heating with potbelly stoves.

Mother nodded, understanding. "It gives off heat all through the night, then. Bet it's cozy in the morning..."

"That's great in the winter. Spring days, when the lawn's still covered with snow, I have to open the windows sometimes. People think I'm crazy when they see lace curtains flapping in the breeze."

☆ ☆ ☆

At another Owego stop, another day, I kept looking at a peculiar umbrella–and–cane stand in the hall. Our host noticed, "Go ahead and touch it, Eupha," he invited. It felt like leather. The base reminded me of a horse's hard hoof. It was lined with enameled tin to hold things.

"Know what it's made of?" I shook my head. "That, my dear, is the foot of a real elephant."

I, too, had been to see the elephant.

CHAPTER 25

What About Harry?

Harry was ready to grab the world by the tail even before I was born. I remember him as an always welcome visitor. He managed to be home for most family reunions. He'd use the guest room or sleep on the couch, and play requests at the piano for hours at a time.

This fascinated me and he knew it. "Come here, sis," he'd beckon, putting the thick unabridged dictionary on a chair at his left. He produced bass chords by rapid rotation of his wrist since his three middle fingers had been truncated by a close encounter with a buzz saw.

Once he heard a tune, he could play it. He never learned to

---

read music well, but all his life, he tuned pianos, played hymns at home funerals, and sang his way to local recognition in barber shop quartets.

He brought us advertising give–aways from whoever was his current employer and tiny cakes of soap from overnight hotels. Because they were from him, I prized, but never wrote in, a vest pocket sized memo book bound in dark brown imitation crinkled leather, stamped "Jantzen Pianos," and an equally small record book for travel expenses — he was a sales-man who got around.

I saved a news picture of dignified, impressive "Black Jack" Pershing, a giant in my eyes. He was Harry's commander in New Mexico as they pursued Pancho Villa, that elusive "Mexican Bandit." Harry's military career was cut short for his horse stumbled in the desert and threw him into cactus whose sharp spines worked themselves deeply into his flesh. He received a medical discharge after spending weeks in the hospital, but experienced a lifetime of irritation and discomfort.

Harry finally returned to the Southern Tier and found his niche with Britton as an agent for Travelers' Insurance, with many customers in the Whitney Point and Bainbridge areas. The company brought out its series of Currier and Ives reproduc-tions on wall calendars and cannily sold them to the agents. Harry had busy holiday seasons as he delivered them and wrote up new and renewal policies as a result. People framed their favorite prints.

Unlike our father, Harry became bald at an early age, and

was somewhat put out when, accompanying Mother and Dad, he was mistaken as Mom's husband. He learned to laugh at this, and at the incongruity of being named Harry, "Which I'm not, except on my chest!"

Harry was, by birth, my brother, but he was more an uncle whom I never knew very well.

Vacationing: Uncles Sam Hill
and Orlie Barton

CHAPTER 26

The Months

from *Coe and Christie Story Hour Reader*
Book Two c.1914

January brings the ice and snow,
    Makes our feet and fingers glow.
February brings St. Valentine, —
    Letters to your house and mine.
March brings breezes very shrill,
    And pussy willows by the rill.
April brings the primrose sweet.
    Tulip and hyacinth — what a treat!
May hangs leaves upon the trees,
    Swaying and swaying in the breeze.
June brings daisies and pink roses,
    Fills our arms with pretty posies.
Hot July brings the cooling showers.
    And many, many fragrant flowers.
August brings the poppies red,
    Sunflowers towering overhead.
September brings the goldenrod.
    On breezy days, just see it nod!
October paints the maple leaves,
    They gayly dance upon the trees.
November brings the chilling blast,
    And then the leaves go whirling fast.
December brings the bright red holly,
    When boys and girls are glad and jolly.

About the Author

Eupha M. Shanly spent her first three–and–a–half decades in New York's Southern Tier — Owego, Vestal, and Binghamton. She has lived in southwestern Ohio since 1976.

The interim years were spent "on the job, wherever," as a wife and mother, librarian, advertising copywriter, newspaper staffer, church secretary, or free–lancer in various states, and in 1961–62, in Kabul, Afganistan.

Vivid recollections of her early years are reinforced by extensive research and correspondence. Some incidents were previously told in a Sunday magazine article, *Growing Up On Hiawatha Island*.